In this WMG Writer's Guide, *USA Today* bestselling author and renowned business blogger Kristine Kathryn Rusch helps guide writers to find the right attitude for a long-term writing career.

The
WMG Writer's Guide
Series

the
write
attitude

A WMG WRITER'S GUIDE

KRISTINE KATHRYN RUSCH

WMGPUBLISHING

The Write Attitude

Published 2015 by WMG Publishing
www.wmgpublishing.com
Cover art © copyright Arturaliev/Dreamstime
Book and cover design copyright © 2015 WMG Publishing
Cover design by Allyson Longueira/WMG Publishing
ISBN-13: 978-1-56146-634-4
ISBN-10: 1-56146-634-4

"Beginners Luck," first appeared as a blog post in Business Musings on kristinekathrynrusch.com, March 18, 2015.

"Believe in Yourself," first appeared as a blog post in The Business Rusch on kristinekathrynrusch.com, October 26, 2011.

"Churning It Out," first appeared as a blog post in Business Musings on kristinekathrynrusch.com, January 7, 2015.

"Controlling the Creatives," first appeared as a blog post in Business Musings on kristinekathrynrusch.com, March 25, 2015.

"Following the Crowd," first appeared as a blog post in Business Musings on kristinekathrynrusch.com, February 4, 2015.

"Getting By," first appeared as a blog post in Business Musings on kristinekathrynrusch.com, March 4, 2015.

"Habits," first appeared as a blog post in The Business Rusch on kristinekathrynrusch.com, May 1, 2013.

"The Importance of Routines," first appeared as a blog post in Business Musings on kristinekathrynrusch.com, March 11, 2015.

"Indispensible," first appeared as a blog post in Business Musings on kristinekathrynrusch.com, February 25, 2015.

"One Phone Call From Our Knees," first appeared as a blog post in The Business Rusch on kristinekathrynrusch.com, April 25, 2012.

"Out! All of You!" first appeared as a blog post in The Business Rusch on kristinekathrynrusch.com, February 20, 2013.

"The Writer You Want to Be," first appeared as a blog post in The Business Rusch on kristinekathrynrusch.com, September 12, 2012.

The Pursuit of Perfection copyright © 2015 by Kristine Kathryn Rusch

Contents

the write attitude

A WMG WRITER'S GUIDE

INTRODUCTION

This book came about—as so many of my nonfiction books do—because someone suggested it. In this case, the man who suggested the book didn't even know he had.

Jason Chen of Storybundle asked me to curate a Storybundle on the craft of writing. For those of you unfamiliar with Storybundle and other websites of its type, the bundles are assembled from the works of various authors. The authors contribute e-books, and those e-books get sold for a special price, often set by the consumer.

In addition to getting a bundle of books generally for less than the price of a single paperback, the consumer can also contribute to a charity at the same time.

I love participating in Storybundle. Over the years, I've done several. And that was a problem.

Jason doesn't like repeating books in various bundles—even though previous bundles are no longer available.

In the fall of 2014, I included a craft book in a bundle curated by Kevin J. Anderson. Normally, I would have put that book—*The Pursuit of Perfection and How It Harms Writers*—into any craft bundle, but I had already done so.

Still, I had time. I decided to write several craft-focused posts on my writing and publishing blog, *Business Musings*. The blog appears on my website every week. I also keep a list of the topics I've covered. Head to my website, kristinekathrynrusch.com, and click on the Business Resources tab. You'll find a lot of information there.

As I started to write the posts, I realized I was writing less about how-to-write than I was about attitudes. Attitude makes the difference between a successful writer and a want-to-be writer.

I don't just mean attitude as in that happy-go-lucky *you-can-do-it!* rah-rah stuff you find in most how to write (or how to do anything) books. I mean the way that a writer should look at her writing, her career, and her life in order to succeed.

Before I go further, I should define a few things.

When I talk about writing, I mean the actual creative part of the process. Creating new words. Playing. Not revision, not rewriting, not all the drudgery stuff your English teacher had you do in high school. If you don't understand why I say creating new words is important but rewriting isn't, then pick up *The Pursuit of Perfection* or follow the links in the Endnotes to read the original posts free on my blog.

When I talk about career, I don't mean hobby. I really don't. And I don't mean something you do while you have a day job. I mean a career in writing that lasts *for decades*, not one that will last maybe five good years before petering out. I've been at this career since I was sixteen, which is (sad to say) nearly forty years. I've had ups and I've had downs, and I've weathered all of them—by having, finding, or rekindling the right attitude.

When I talk about life, I mean the stuff you do in addition to your writing. It's all part of the package that is you. Your life informs your writing. Your writing can intrude on your life, if you let it. Your life *will* intrude on your writing at times.

The key is to make writing *part* of your life, but not your entire life.

If you want to be a career writer—someone who has decades of writing and publishing—then you must find the right balance for you. You will give up things and you will also find things because of the writing.

Because I assembled this book from blog posts, the book is anecdotal. After I finished the initial posts, I thumbed through what I had written in five years of blogging on writing and publishing, and found some other posts that were, in some ways, even closer to the idea of this book.

I decided not to cut the posts much. I didn't want this to be a standard how-to book, only filled with advice and *shoulds*. I think *shoulds* are deadly to the writer.

Instead, I left the posts mostly intact because they were written in the moment, and they show how I grappled with large problems that came my way.

I wrote these through serious illness (I nearly died in the spring of 2012), the loss of friends and family, the near-loss of my career, and the start of several businesses (not just writing-related). I share some ups here as well as some downs.

I am rather amazed at how clearly my attitude comes through these posts. The attitude—my strong desire to write and to remain the writer I want to be—informs almost every word.

A few other things to clear up here, for those of you who've never come to my blog. I'm married to another writer, Dean Wesley Smith, who writes both fiction and nonfiction. We've been together nearly thirty years, through ups and downs. He also blogs about writing and publishing at deanwesleysmith.com. I mention him and his blog a lot.

We co-own several businesses, including three retail stores (at last count), and a publishing company. Yet we make most of our personal income through writing.

We have owned a lot of businesses over our years together, as well as several businesses before we met each other. So you'll see that many of my posts are business-oriented, even when I talk about craft, because business is how I think about things.

I also edit. I'm currently editing projects for WMG Publishing, Baen Books, and Kobo. I used to edit *The Magazine of Fantasy & Science Fiction*. I've won awards for both my editing and my writing.

And once upon a time, I was the news director of a radio station.

Yet through it all, writing sustained me and outearned everything else I did. When the other jobs (or the other businesses) got in the way of writing, I jettisoned them.

Sounds easy. It was often hard.

Some of those difficulties inform this book. Some will have to wait until another book.

I hope you find a lot to think about here. I organized everything to move you from setting up your writing habits to dealing with the outside world to remembering why you like writing.

Most of all, though, I hope you enjoy the book.

And if you have questions, you can find me, every week, blogging about something at kristinekathrynrusch.com.

Attitude affects everything that we do, from the moment we wake up until the moment we go to bed. Our attitude directs how we approach our writing as well.

Choices are decisions, and decisions often fall into the yes-or-no category. When we make something a habit, we remove the decision. We no longer give ourselves the choice to write or not to write. We make it a habit. Here's more on habits, from a post in 2013.

CHAPTER ONE

HABITS

As of Tuesday, around 10 p.m., I finished the first draft of *Street Justice: A Smokey Dalton Novel.* I would have finished on Monday, but Dean and I have been dealing with some serious business matters for the past ten days, and on Monday, we had to do real-life business things that involved people, not computers or mentally time-traveling back to 1970. And we certainly couldn't make things up, or we would have made some pretty serious mistakes.

I get very focused at the end of a book, and I speed up because I want to finish and move to the next project. I have a lot of next projects. I have three short stories due in the next two weeks. I need to go over a first draft of a different novel, and add a few things that I thought of later. Sometimes I leave novels to "cool" and then the subconscious tosses in the missing elements. Since I usually write out of order, this habit generally works to my advantage.

I'm leaving *Street Justice* to cool while I finish up those tasks. And as I'm doing those, I'll also write at least two more blog posts for the Business Rusch, several smaller items that WMG Publishing needs, and maybe a mystery story (since the three I owe are science fiction (2) and romance (1), and I'd like to get to this great mystery idea that's been hanging fire for weeks now).

Why am I burdening you with all of this? For two reasons. First, I planned to write a long and involved post tonight about advertising, royalty statements, and book distribution. In fact, I started it in the middle of the night Monday when I couldn't sleep. But I'm tired enough that I worry I wouldn't do my best work on the blog, so I'm going to put it off until later.

The other reason? Some of you know that for the last ten days or so of April, Dean was writing a novel from start to finish. In fact, he was writing a novel and blogging about it at the same time. (Those blog posts became his nonfiction book *How To Write a Novel in Ten Days*.)

We're always writing, and we're usually writing novels at the same time, but it's rare for us both to be going at top speed at the same time. Generally, one of us serves as backup for the other, making sure the other person eats properly, gets up from the desk enough, and gets enough sleep.

We couldn't really watch each other's backs this time, and it led to some interesting things that I didn't quite realize until today.

Today, I grabbed the battered and scratched grocery list that had been sitting on the dining room table for weeks, and headed to the grocery store. Usually I do the shopping and the cooking because I have so many food allergies that it's just easier (and less time consuming) for me to handle this stuff.

I go once a week, grab enough to last, replenish what we used up, and bring it all home. Dean carries his weight in other ways. He does the dishes if I cook, and he handles repairs/lightbulbs/etc.

For the past two weeks, maybe three, I didn't go to the store. I ran out of time. I also ran out of time to cook. Fortunately, I cook too much food most of the time and freeze the suitable leftovers. In March, I actually had to buy more food storage containers because we hadn't been eating anything frozen. I wondered if our eating habits had changed.

Au contraire. I did not realize I was storing up for April.

All of last week, we ate what I had stored. We also ate through our extras. We almost ran out of tea, which, believe me, almost never happens in my house. (Some wag at the grocery store today looked in my cart at the four boxes of cereal and said, "Wow. Someone in your house likes Raisin Bran." I didn't tell him I was stocking back up.)

Getting extra food and freezing leftovers aren't habits that came from my Depression-era parents (even though Mother did try to instill in me the virtues of using *everything*, a lesson I still ignore). These habits come from decades of freelancing.

Back in the early days, I learned to buy in bulk because checks came irregularly. I could get through the lean times with extra boxes of cereal and lots of frozen homemade food.

Later, though, those same habits became important in a two-writer household for months like the one we just went through. We don't have a housekeeper or a secretary. We have to keep track of things ourselves and can't farm it out to an assistant. (I suppose we could afford one, but that person would be lurking in my home and breathing my air, and at some point, I would just have to kill him. No, I'm not the most rational person when I'm working. I'm a writer. Why would you expect otherwise?)

Without an assistant, Dean and I muddle through. Most of the time, even a two-novel finish isn't as complicated as last week because, on top of the dual writing sessions, we also had to handle some heavy-duty business stuff that took hours out of our days. Despite my vow to eat healthier in 2013, a vow I've mostly kept, I ate too many lunches from Burger King because I'd run out of everything easy to fix in the house, and I knew if I went to the grocery store, I'd lose too much writing time, a fact borne out today, when I lost two hours in the aisles at Safeway.

The frozen meals do help, though. We eat less crap when we have frozen homemade food. And it's something we've done for years. We have a lot of habits that have simply become ingrained, habits I didn't entirely realize others lacked until Dean blogged about writing a novel in ten days.[1]

Writers asked a lot of questions in the comments, so while he was writing the book, Dean also did a lot of mythbusting.

One myth in particular stood out for me. Most writers seemed to believe that you had to spend a large chunk of time at the computer to write anything of value.

That can't be further from the truth. In fact, large chunks of time at the computer *harm* a writer. They rarely help one.

I've always wondered how so many writers develop carpal tunnel syndrome and other repetitive stress injuries from their writing. When Dean and I teach, we always stress that a writer needs to have her workplace properly set up. I blogged about that early in *The Freelancer's Survival Guide*. Your work space should be set up for your body style, not for someone else's. I also tell writers to get up every hour or so.

I learned this one quickly. I am incredibly restless—so restless, in fact, that when a doctor ordered me to stay off my feet after I broke a bone in my left foot, I found it nearly impossible to take that advice. I was used to getting up every twenty minutes or so to go do something. I had no idea I was that restless until that particular injury.

But I also trained my body to move. I did so with tea and water. Before each writing session, I drink a little water. Then I bring a cup of tea with me into the office, and sip as I work. Eventually, my body demands that I get up and after a while, I can no longer ignore that command—even if my characters are all about to die in icky horrible ways. Even if I have just gotten a great idea and need to get it all down *now*. Even if I have finally figured out that missing piece to the plot puzzle. I still have to get up, and walk to the bathroom, then have another drink of water, maybe make another cup of tea, and head back, shaking my arms a little as I do so, making sure I stretch a bit, and avoiding repetitive stress injury.

I only had one such injury, and I got that in the late 1980s, when I worked as a secretary. I sat at a desk set up for someone seven inches taller than me, and eventually, I paid for that. It didn't matter how many times I got up. I still got hurt, and vowed never again.

Dean gets up every hour or so as well. The fact that we both do this has led to another habit. We learned to write in small increments. We often write two hundred words in fifteen minutes, then get up and do something else. On Sundays, before our weekly writer lunch, I can usually manage only about twenty minutes of actual writing before we leave. I generally get 600-800 words done in that time, mostly because I know I will lose most of my afternoon to socializing.

What these short bursts mean is that we write a lot more than most people. If I waited for long stretches of time to write, I'd still be finishing *Street Justice*. I had several hours to work yesterday, but no time on Monday, five hours in snatches on Sunday, a long stretch on Saturday, and four stolen nonconsecutive hours on Friday. If I look back at April, which was a busy month for business and other things that had nothing to do with writing, I see only ten days with long stretches of time. I wrote most of *Street Justice* in April. I'd only be about a hundred pages in if I wrote like most of the commenters on Dean's blog.

As readers of the blog learned, Dean writes that way as well. He writes a bit, does something else, then writes some more. He gets thousands of words done per day by doing that.

So do I.

The other thing we both do is we each have a dedicated writing computer. I gave a live interview online a few years ago, and got to see the running comments from others on the message board. They made fun of me as a Luddite for making certain that my writing computer did not have e-mail or Twitter or any wireless connectivity. I don't have a phone in my office either, or a television or my iPad. No novels except my own. Research books are all the way across the room, out of easy grasp.

No distractions. None.

When I sit at this desk, I write. I do nothing else. Because I'm so firm about this, I know that the moment I sit down, I am going to work. The habit becomes reality. I'm already thinking of the next scene as I walk through the office door. I review a little, and then start typing. And I do that until my timer goes off or nature calls.

Yes, I set a timer. If I only have a half an hour for writing, I set the timer for twenty-five minutes. Why twenty-five minutes? Because that way, I can finish my thought or the scene or make notes for the next writing session.

It's a habit I learned when I was training myself to write.

I used to think starting was hard. Then I realized that I was just easily distracted. I took away all of my distractions, and set an obnoxious alarm across the room. Then I vowed not to move from my writing desk until that damn alarm went off.

I'm easily bored. Without books nearby or television or even a radio, I had a choice: I could either sit and stare into space or I could write something. I ended up writing something. And after weeks of this, I could ditch the alarm.

Now I use a timer just to make sure I'm not late to whatever appointment I have. (And those of you who know me, stop laughing. Yes, I know I'm still late at times.)

The physical habits feed the writing. If I hadn't been getting up every hour or so for the last three decades, I would no longer be a writer. I'd be in traction.

If I believed I needed large chunks of time to write, I would have written maybe an eighth of what I've written over those three decades.

If I hadn't figured out how to manage real world things, like grocery shopping and cooking, I wouldn't finish novels as quickly.

Dean and I didn't eat poorly last week, but we didn't eat well, either. I managed to get some exercise, although not as much as usual. If one of us had been finishing a novel instead of both of us, that person probably would have eaten better and gotten more time for exercise.

But we were keeping the household together kinda and managing pretty well. Just like we would have if we lived alone or the other person was out of town.

The habits kept us fed, kept us producing words regularly, and kept us injury free.

We're both tired tonight, which is why I'm going to roust him from his office now. We're going to go do something relaxing.

But we'll both be back at it tomorrow.

Because writing is our job, and we treat it that way. Even down to the little things, the smallest of habits.

Writing demystified. That's what Dean was doing last week.

Which is why I urge you to all go read his posts on that novel. (Or pick up *How To Write A Novel in Ten Days*.)

Me? I have to get rid of some tea, post this blog, and go do something fun—whatever that may be.

From habits to routines. Routines create habits. Habits foster routines. I've known this forever, and yet I didn't blog about it until 2015. Sometimes the most essential thing becomes such a habit that we don't even notice it. I didn't notice the routines until I was out of my routine for more than a week.

CHAPTER TWO

THE IMPORTANCE OF ROUTINES

We just finished the anthology workshop, the largest workshop we do in person. Forty-six attendees, eight instructors, seven days, and 250 manuscripts to read and discuss. All of the attendees are professional writers in one capacity or another (technical writers, nonfiction writers, fiction writers), so the manuscript quality was high—often award-quality.

Oh, the discussions. Oh, the fights (among the instructors). Oh, the laughter.

Yes, we had fun.

And now, with deep gratitude, I return to my writing routine.

The first two days after the workshop involved catch-up, a sudden rewrite, some small promotion for this month's book release, and this thing called sleep. Today (Wednesday) is the first day I'm even approximating my usual schedule—much to the joy of my office cat, Galahad. (By Friday of last week, he took to standing in the door of my office and yelling at me as loudly as he could. He's on my lap and purring as I type this [and yes, that means my typing posture has gone all to hell].)

Galahad isn't the only one who is joyful. I'm bouncing around like a kid at Christmas, despite a lingering tiredness, a possible cold (allergies?), and constant interruptions from other people's emergencies. My routine enables my writing productivity. My routine also takes away one aspect of my work day—the stress of time management.

I felt that stress during the workshop. I had left some reading for the middle of the week, assuming I would have time for it. I didn't, but I had to get it done, which meant that the time came from the eight hours scheduled for sleep.

I had also vowed (to myself) to maintain my daily run, but I ran a route I'd never tried before. (I ran home for lunch.) The first two days were all about clock-checking. *Am I late? Will I have time to shower, change, and eat lunch before my ride shows up?* A few days were dicey, and then I got the hang of it—about the time I was headed back into my regular routine.

In my regular routine, I know if I linger too long at dinner, I will sacrifice my evening writing session. My brain shuts down around 10 or 11 every night. I plan for 10 rather than try to push for 11, because that way, if I'm particularly energetic, I feel like I've gained something rather than merely achieving my goal.

If I get started later than usual, I lose the all-important first session where I set my daily pattern. Often, I don't tend to e-mail and everything that piled up overnight until I've completed my first writing session. That way, it's harder to knock me off schedule.

And so on and so on and so on.

The routine enables the writing, not the other way around.

For almost two years, Dean has blogged nightly about his writing routine,[2] pointing out to writers around the world that a writing career isn't about *pushing*. It's about a regular routine, almost clockwork in its repetitiveness. If you don't understand what

I mean, I urge you to take a look—and to make sure you read dozens of the blog posts, rather than one or two.

Even when Dean gets off-routine, he's honest about it. And you can see in his numbers just how badly going off-routine impacts his productivity.

Going off-routine hurts mine too. I had eight writing things scheduled for Monday. Instead, I spent most of the time cleaning up messes from the week before. Those eight things moved to Tuesday, along with Tuesday's schedule. Again, I dealt with other people's emergencies.

Today, I finally got to routine, and before I started writing this blog, I checked off six of the original eight things. The blog is the seventh. The eighth will move to Thursday, along with the rest of today's items.

I suspect I'll be shuffling due dates and projects for another week, even though I had planned around the workshop. The workshop didn't cause the backlog as much as the loss of Monday and Tuesday did.

In *The Freelancer's Survival Guide*, I have an entire section on scheduling. (You can find it on my website for free[3] or in the *Guide* or in the short book called *Time Management*.) I reread this section before I started this post, and was rather stunned to realize I never talked about routine. Let me define terms here:

A schedule is two-pronged.

First, a schedule includes calendar items. Your day job (if you have one). Your days off. The vacation you'll take with you and your family. The writers conferences you'll attend. The evenings you need to take for your daughter's violin concerts. The lunch you have every week with your fellow writers. And so on.

Second, a schedule includes your writing (and publishing) deadlines. It shouldn't matter if these deadlines are self-imposed or imposed from the outside (by a traditional publisher, for example). A deadline should be hard and fast. You don't miss the deadline. In the *Freelancer's Guide*, I show techniques for counting backwards so that you can find the right amount of time to get the work done—without pushing the deadline.

When I talk *schedule*, I'm not talking about *routine*.

Routine is the way that you shape your day. Every day.

From the time you get up in the morning to the length of your first writing session, your routine should have some kind of pattern to it. Dean posts his daily routine on his blog.

Here's mine:

I get up around 11, take care of household stuff, and check the e-mail for emergencies. That can take anywhere from one hour to two hours, depending if there is an emergency or not.

I have a snack when I get up, but I eat a full breakfast after that one-to-two-hour period. If I'm running late (two hours), I eat quickly and drink my tea at my desk. If I'm on the normal schedule (one hour), I linger a bit.

Then I write for two sessions, with a longer e-mail/business break in between. I go on my run, eat lunch, feed the cats, and return to work for another session (or two) before cooking dinner.

After dinner, I return to my office for a last session or two, depending on how tired I am. When I'm finished, I do any reading I need to do. I join Dean for a little television, then come back to my reading chair to read for enjoyment for two hours before going to bed with enough time to spare so that I can get eight hours of rest.

Day in, day out.

Twice a week, I change the routine. Once a week, I go to a series of business meetings. I try to schedule other disruptive things on that day as well, like doctor's appointments, podcast interviews, dinner with friends, car repairs, etc.

The other thing that alters my routine is our professional writers lunch on Sunday, which I try not to miss. I can miss it if I'm pushing a deadline. (Yes, despite my tough talk, I occasionally push a deadline—and regret it as I struggle to get my work done.) I schedule writing that requires less concentration for that day or maybe I do some business things, because the lunch can be really disruptive.

And that's it.

The rest of the time, I'm following the routine I listed above. I know how many writing hours I have in the week and how much work I have. If I stay in routine, I can accurately estimate what I'm capable of writing and finishing and when I'm capable of finishing it.

Without the routine, I couldn't estimate accurately.

But the routine is more than that. It's also a structure that requires very little thought. When I go to my office at the usual time, my brain has already started to work on the current project even before I sit down. I'm ready to work right from the start.

The routine also organizes those around me. They know that when I'm in my writing office, I'm unavailable. Unless I'm between major projects, I don't participate in social events on the five "regular" work days. Conversely, I'm pretty easy to reach at some point in the day, if the other person is patient.

I do set up routines when I travel or when I do events in town, like the workshop. Usually I try to plan those out ahead of time, although I wasn't able to during this workshop. I do a lot of writing on planes, a lot of business while in the hustle and bustle of airports, and a lot of research while people-watching in strange environments.

In other words, routines are essential to my process.

Most effective writers have routines. I know that many of you who read this have day jobs and less writing time than I have. The day jobs give you structure. Writers who get a lot done have a set time after or before their day jobs for writing. Even an hour per day is enough to finish a lot of pages.

If you don't have a routine, if you're waiting for that elusive muse or if you're "too busy," take the time to write down everything you do for about two weeks. You'll find some spare time in there. It might only be fifteen minutes in the course of a day, but even fifteen minutes should get you one page per day. One page per day for 365 days per year is a novel. Take weekends off, and you'll still get a lot of writing done.

So here I am, sneezing my way through today's routine. The cat has moved to his evening nap spot, and I'm about to move to another project—with an hour in my regular routine to spare.

Life is good.

Nice to be back in routine.

I designed the early part of this book to get you to your writing office. Now that you're there, let's make sure you actually write. Most of what we do as writers takes place in our heads. And most of what we do to stop ourselves also takes place in our heads.

Sometimes, something as simple as the words we use to describe what we do will stop us from performing at our best. This blog post, from 2015, points out one of the most deadly phrases...

CHAPTER THREE

CHURNING IT OUT

Toward the end of a pretty good *Entertainment Weekly*[4] article about the romance side of the publishing industry, this sentence appears:

> *[Bella Andre]'s a naturally fast writer—on average she churns out four to six books a year—and she released the first one in June 2011.*

Before we get to the reason I'm telling you about that sentence, let me say one thing that might or might not be related: There's a slight snobby tone to *EW*'s romance article. What's *that* all about? The magazine's called **Entertainment** *Weekly*, not *The New York Times Book Review. EW* sings the praises of *The Walking Dead* and video games, and everything in between, for heaven's sake, but somehow *romance* fiction doesn't meet the high standards of *entertainment*?

Sorry. I had to get that off my chest.

As I said, the article, "A Billion-Dollar Affair," by Karen Valby, appeared in the October 24th issue, and did cover the romance industry pretty well.

So why am I objecting to that single sentence?

I'm not, really. It's a common sentence from any media that covers books. And I'm not even objecting to the entire sentence. Bella Andre does write fast by most writers' standards, and she does so comfortably.

What I'm objecting to is the phrase "churned out."

It's become a cliché. Any writer who writes fast "churns out" material. Or she "cranks out" or "pounds out" whatever it is that she writes. Because clearly, no writer who writes fast can *think* about what she writes.

There are other implications in that phrase. The material "churned out" isn't very good. Anything "churned out" is an exact copy of what has come before. It has no real value, primarily because of the speed with which the writer "churns out" the material.

In the olden days of traditional publishing, those of us who "churned out" a lot of books did so under a lot of pen names. Here's how it worked in my case: Kristine Kathryn Rusch might, at best, put out two books per year; Kris Nelscott one every two years; and Kristine Grayson one every six months.

Most reviewers never noticed all the short stories or blog posts or nonfiction. Only a handful of people (including my agents back when I was stupid enough to hire them) knew that I wrote under other pen names as well.

While reading a midlist thriller novel in bed one night several years ago, I laughed so hard that I woke Dean up. What made me laugh? The author's bio, which stated that the byline of the novel I was reading was a pen name for a "well-known #1 *New York*

Times bestselling author." Ballsy and hysterical. That writer wrote so many books that his publisher refused to publish them all *under the author's bestselling name.*

Or maybe the publisher never got a chance. Because I later discovered who the author in question was (and that's why I'm not naming the book here), and discovered that the author had nearly a dozen pen names, and kept them all quiet—except for that coy little bio for at least one of them.

In the opening to *Bag of Bones*, Stephen King writes that his main character, a bestselling novelist, kept one novel in the drawer for every novel he published, since his publisher was demanding that he publish no more than one book per year.

Think about this, people: How many other industries that have megaselling products demand that the producer of popular, high-quality material *slow down*? What happened to providing the consumers with what they wanted?

When Nora Roberts started out, she was fortunate to begin with Harlequin, which could publish as many books as she produced. She stayed with Harlequin even after she moved to a bigger publisher (Bantam) for a once-per-year hardcover, which then became a once-per-year hardcover and twice-a-year mass market paper, and then became twice-a-year hardcovers and three-times-a-year mass market paper, and finally, she had a big fight with Harlequin, and started up the J.D. Robb pen name (twice per year) and her publisher (by then, Putnam) threw in the towel. The publisher finally agreed that *Nora* could put out a lot of books. But not the publisher's other writers.

Nora Roberts' speed didn't matter to that publisher because the publisher had no expectation of quality based on the genre. As we all know, and *Entertainment Weekly's* snobby tone confirms, romance is trash anyway. No one expects quality fiction from writers who crank out cookie-cutter books for women.

You think I'm kidding, right? I'm not. I'm old enough to have read the trade journals as romance got its start as a genre, as the Romance Writers of America fought for recognition from publishers, as romance readers slowly realized that they were marketing force that had a lot of clout.

Romance has a lot of respect now compared to thirty years ago—and still writers see phrases like "churned out" and that slightly school-boyish tone that every Literary Critic uses when discussing romance.

It's about love and mushy stuff. It can't be *good*. It might include kissing and touching and actual irony-free emotion. Anyone can churn out that crap if they put their minds to it. But most people are sensible enough to want respectability instead of... whatever it is that these romance people have.

Oh, yeah. Money.

And readers.

Who actually like the books.

I have taken exception to that snobbish attitude for my entire career. I've written essay after essay about it in all kinds of journals and magazines. I've written some business blogs on it too.

Back when I was writing those essays, the attitude was merely annoying. Savvy writers could get past it with the judicious use of pen names, and make not just a living, but a substantial living. As in earning mid-six figures or more, simply by hiding the fact that the fast writers wrote more than one book per year.

That snobbish attitude has always been harmful to writers who wanted to make a living. But in my mind, that snobbery always went hand-in-hand with a desire to be recognized over a desire to have a full-time writing career. The writers who wanted to make a living figured out how to handle the respectability argument while "churning out" a lot of books. The writers who wanted respectability and labored over each word never left their day jobs.

Now, however, that snobbish attitude has become actively harmful to writers. Most of the ways that books sell to readers have broken down. The traditional publishing systems have lost their impact. The old-fashioned way that publishers advertised books—that one-size-fits-all method—no longer works. Bookstores don't window titles much anymore, if a reader can find a brick-and-mortar bookstore that sells new titles within driving distance of home.[5]

Because books are available all the time rather than for only a few months, readers pay less attention to release dates than ever before. Readers have always *read* a book when they felt like it, and not a moment sooner. But in the past, readers had to *buy* the book when they saw it, because they might never find a copy again.

So, even if readers didn't read the book for a year or more, readers still had to buy it in that limited time window.

Not any longer. Readers can make a note of the title, realize it's been published, and buy it days or hours or minutes before reading it. That really changes the way that the publishing industry markets books—or it should.

It hasn't yet, entirely, anyway. But the industry is starting to get a clue.

Event books, the ones that publishers convinced the media to promote, are no longer events. The numbers to become a bestseller[6] are much, much lower than they were as little as seven years ago.

Lists matter, but less and less as readers discover their books in other ways.

And one of the major ways that readers discover a book? E-mail alerts or notifications that scroll across the reader's favorite online retailing site—alerts and notifications *tailored to that reader*.

No longer do we all get notification of the top five books on *The New York Times* bestseller list. Now, we get science fiction (if that's what we read) or romance or mystery. We get notifications about our favorite author's latest book, not the latest release from some author whose work we would never, ever, ever read.

The notifications come from bots designed by the retailers. What provokes those bots to let a reader know about an author? Publication of her latest work. The bots always send readers a note that an author they have bought before (through that retailer) has released a new book.

The reader might not buy that book immediately, but the book might go on a wish list. It might be put in reserve until the reader has the cash to order or the time to read.

Another change in the way people buy books also has to do with unlimited availability. All readers indulged in binge reading of a new-to-them author, but in the past, that binge reading was combined with treasure hunting.

Whenever I discovered a new writer whose work I liked, I'd read what was easily available, then I'd go to the library to see what it had. Libraries never had the complete oeuvre because, like bookstores, they have limited shelf space. So I'd dig through every used bookstore in every town I visited until I got each and every book by that author.

Or as close to each and every book as I could get.

Other readers did the same.

Now, readers can order every book that a favorite author has written, whether that author has written five books or hundreds. That fear writers have, the fear that readers won't respect the work if it doesn't take years to complete, is silly when looked at from a reader's perspective.

Readers want to escape from their lives for a few hours. They might want to read a beautiful well-written slow-moving literary novel or they might want to read a fast-paced hard-to-believe thriller. But readers want the book when they're ready to relax. If they liked that book, they want another by the same author. The author becomes a known quantity, and the reader wants more.

Binge-reading has become an all-consuming activity, just like binge-watching. And the best way to get noticed as a writer is to publish enough to enable your readers to binge for a weekend.

But the idea of writing a lot is the opposite of the way that most writers are trained. Writers are told to slow down, think about every word, consider every sentence. Writers are taught to forget story because story is something that hack writers do.

Hack writers can "churn" out words because words are unimportant to them.

Real writers write so slowly that they might only compose a paragraph per day.

Real writers who have day jobs and who still believe myths spouted in the 19th century.

Real 19th-century writers who are still read today, like Charles Dickens or Louisa May Alcott, got paid by the word, so they wrote a lot of words, for a lot of publications. These writers wrote fast *long hand*, and they "churned out" a lot of stories we no longer read.

But they also "churned out" stories that all of us still read.

That little phrase, "churned out," holds so much disrespect. Deadly disrespect, because writers who hear that phrase—and use it themselves—won't be able to survive in this new world.

The 21st century is not leisurely, although we have more leisure time than ever. Can you remember the name of the "important" literary novel of five years ago? Ten? Without looking it up? I didn't think so.

Yet, I can still name the important literary novels of forty years ago, because they got all the press, and I do mean *all* the press.

It's impossible to get all of the press now. The best way to get attention is to give your readers what they want. If they like your work, they want more of it.

If they want more of it, the only person who can give them more is you.

And the only way to do that is to write a lot, whatever that means for you.

One sure way to teach yourself to write at a comfortable pace is to clean up your language. Watch every word. Make sure you're using the right phrase—when you're *talking* about writing.

Clean "churned out" from your vocabulary. Don't say you "cranked out" a novel. Don't apologize for writing fast. Don't tell anyone how long it took to finish a novel.

Write and release.

The only people who judge fiction writers for how fast they write are people for whom reading isn't something they do for enjoyment but for prestige. They want to impress others with their literary acumen.

I don't know about you, but I want readers who get lost in the story, not readers who have already determined that I'm a hack because I don't write at the proper speed or in the proper genre or with the proper attention to language.

Enjoy your writing. Take as much—or as little—time as you like to compose your stories.

Because *how* you created the story doesn't matter. How much readers enjoy the story does. Readers don't care if it took you one week to write that story or fifteen years. All readers want is escape.

And it's your job to provide it.

The flip side of writing fast is doing just enough to make yourself feel like a real writer. I hadn't realized how engrained "getting by" is in our culture until I had an experience with three separate employees in 2014, employees who did the minimal amount of work and expected somehow to receive kudos for doing so. Those employees got me wondering about writers and their attitudes.

I wrote this blog post after that experience, but sat on it for a while. I talked to other professional writers about their opinions on the topic, and we all agreed that even in writing, some folks just try to get by...

CHAPTER FOUR

GETTING BY

Here's an anecdote those of you who have faithfully read my *Business Rusch* blog or *The Freelancer's Survival Guide* have encountered before. I apologize for the repetition, but the context needs to be here. I will bring this anecdote around to writing and freelancing further on in this piece.

One-hundred-and-fifty-thousand years ago (or the early 1980s, whichever makes me seem older), I got a job at a textbook publishing company. I came in as the lowest of the low, an editorial assistant—in other words, a secretary with a fancy title that made me seem more important than I was.

I was barely out of college and the best thing I had going for me was that I knew how to turn on a computer. (Seriously, these people had had a new computer sitting idly because no one could find the *on* switch.) We did everything by hand or by typewriter, and for the bulk of my time there, that computer gathered dust.

I had come from freelancing. My (soon-to-be ex-) husband and I owned a failing business, and we were broke. So I got a full-time job to pay the bills.

Day One, I got trained by the woman I was replacing. Day Two, I came in and did everything I had been assigned to do within thirty minutes. My boss, the wonderful Editor Greg, was startled that I finished so quickly. He double-checked me, found out I had done everything right, and gave me more to do. Still and all, I was done with my tasks by noon.

With Editor Greg's permission, I read a book all afternoon. The book was one of the company's textbooks, but Editor Greg thought that it might be useful if I knew the product.

Day Three, same thing.

Day Four, the other secretaries—I mean, editorial assistants—waylaid me as I came into work. They explained in no uncertain terms that I had to make my thirty minutes of work stretch throughout the 8 hours, or I would make every other editorial assistant look bad.

I was baffled. I said, "Why would I want to do that? I hate being bored. And if there's stuff to be done, I'll do it."

They said stuff about camaraderie and supporting your fellow employees and *helping them keep their jobs, for heaven's sake.* And I shrugged and walked away. I continued to do thirty minutes of work in thirty minutes. A month or two into the job, I had read every book in the place and was getting ready to read everything in the files (I did that at a real estate job I had in college—and oh, boy, did I learn stuff) when I realized that our personal financial situation had improved.

I went back to freelancing, earned a lot more money than I did in that crazy-making job, and moved on.

I often talk about those secretaries in astonishment. I thought they were anomalies. Even though a good friend of mine—a very good friend of mine—spent his entire career at a government job that, he said, required him to do eight hours of work in a forty-hour week. He stretched those eight hours over five days, then added in another eight hours in those five days for good measure, and became the most productive person in his department.

He kept that job even though he got sick after every trip he took to an SF convention (generally one per month). He took tons of vacation time and personal days, and he still got promoted and treated well there—*because he was the most productive person in his office.*

I never put A and B together, not really, except to make silly jokes about the things government employees could get away with. But other friends who had corporate jobs would tell me about the folks in their offices who, no matter what anyone tried, never really did much.

Those folks showed up, shuffled papers, and went home.

After that textbook publishing experience, I stopped hiring out as a secretary for part-time work. (For a while anyway. Years later, I moved to Oregon, and was desperate for any part-time work. Then I got hired by a wonderful man [still a friend] who let me leave when I finished the tasks assigned me.) For most of my early working life, part-time work I got to augment my freelance income was as a waitress.

Waitresses in busy restaurants can't slack off. If you do, you get fired. Or, if your bosses really don't care, you don't make money. Because other (good) waiters and waitresses will take your tables—and your tips. By the time I was out of high school, I could handle an entire Country Kitchen restaurant at breakfast by myself (with the assistance of someone to bus tables) and still get customers in and out of the restaurant within an hour.

And I had fun.

Why am I telling you this?

Because one of the things I learned in 2014 is that a lot of employees get by.

Dean and I own or co-own eight different businesses—not all of them to do with publishing. Generally speaking, we're good at hiring people and for the most part, over the years, we have hired excellent folk. We have a good staff of people right now—people who work hard, care a lot, and do an excellent job.

Dean and I have hired and fired people throughout our adult lives, and also generally speaking, we tend to avoid the get-by folks. We get rid of them fast when we accidentally hire them.

How do we accidentally hire them?

They present well. They present as smart and talented and (sometimes) misunderstood. In their (excellent) interviews, they complain that they were in the wrong job. Sometimes, given their résumés, it seems like they actually *were* in the wrong job.

While the get-by folks talk a good game, they don't perform well. After their training is complete, they can't seem to meet deadlines or get work done. There's always a reason.

Some get-by folks, the ones who've been in the work force for a long time, find ways to get other people to do the work for them or they meet their deadlines (just barely) with shoddy work, complaining that the task was hard and almost impossible to do in the time allowed.

When you're a small business owner, chances are you've done the task yourself before hiring someone to take it off your hands. And unlike managers at corporations who supervise people whose jobs they aren't as familiar with, you *know* that the excuses are just excuses.

I hate it when we hire a get-by person. Because they're often extremely nice human beings who are fun to be around. But they aren't good employees.

As you can tell from the mentions above, we had to deal with get-by situations at our many businesses in 2014. While dealing with the aftermath of the get-by situations (and learning just how much never got done), I had a realization about writers.

There are writers who get by.

I've always known that, but I hadn't given it a lot of thought until the indie publishing revolution. Throughout my entire career, I've known writers who take five years to write a book (or a year to write a short story!), writers who never try freelancing because they can't get their production up, writers who can't seem to finish anything after the first few books.

I always thought, ah, it's their critical voice that's on too loud, or they really don't want to become a writer, or they have some other interest that's more important.

I never thought—I never realized—that a goodly percentage of these writers are simply folks who get by. These writers figure out how to game the system at their jobs. They do like my very good friend did at his job; they seem productive when they are not.

Unlike my very good friend, many get-by people seem to believe their own hype. They seem to think there's a way around everything, that everyone else does this, and that successful people aren't people who work hard but are people who know how to play the game well.

Does this sound familiar?

There are blogs everywhere on how to manipulate Amazon's algorithm to make a book a bestseller. There are writers who cringe when you tell them the best way to sell your first book is to write a second. There are writers who simply do not believe that writing the next book (and the next and the next) is more important than promoting the only book.

Honestly, I hadn't understood that mindset until I thought about the Get-By People. They have made entire careers about doing a lot of initial work to impress their employer, and then skating on that work for as long as possible. Part of the skate is a gift for hype that makes the initial work seem more important than it actually is.

You see, they say, it's *hard* to write a novel. Terribly, terribly, terribly hard. The writers suffered as they wrote. The fact that they finished that novel is very, very, very important. These writers should be rewarded for their very hard, very important work. We should all recognize just how much effort these writers put into that novel, and we should respond with sales and accolades.

I never understood that point of view from a non-writerly perspective until this year. I thought it was just something weird that writers did, until I started to talk to others who have dealt in their jobs with the Get-By People.

Expecting recognition for a minimal amount of work is a get-by attitude.

Why do I call writing one novel a minimal amount of work? Because I'm mean or a show-off or a hack or freakishly productive?

No, because I know writers who have long-term careers. Most of us never talk about our productivity. Most of us never talk about how many hours we spend at the computer. As Dean often says, we are successful because we work harder than everyone else.

There are excellent employees in the world, people who put in extra hours or who are "freakishly productive" by filling their days with actual work rather than talking about movies or surfing the web.

(Are you at work right now? Is it your lunch break? Or are you supposed to be working? Or is this scheduled free time? Do you feel guilty yet?)

Some weeks I work harder than those excellent employees. But often I match them in productivity. I had just not seen them in action until the past few years.

Dean, on the other hand, works harder than anyone I've ever met. He's a whiz at getting a lot done in a little bit of time. He's more productive than I am—and I often feel like a Get-By Person in comparison.

But back to that one-novel thing.

It is an accomplishment to finish your first novel. Go celebrate. Most wannabe writers never finish a novel. They may not ever finish a short story. They talk the good talk, but they don't put in the work.

When you finish your first novel, you have taken that first step toward being a professional writer. But from the perspective of career writers, people who've been at it for years, you're a baby who has toddled over to your parents for the very first time.

Yep, it's an accomplishment worthy of cake and videos and applause.

Now, time to emulate that toddler and learn to run.

These days, most indie writers expect that first novel to be a success. I expected my first (real) novel to be a success as well. We all write because we know we're brilliant, because the world was just waiting for our wisdom, because we have done something Mankind Has Never Seen Before.

Then those of us who want careers get over ourselves and move onto the next novel, and the next, and the next, and the next.

Right now, the Get-By People who wrote that first novel, gamed Amazon's algorithms, and tried to convince everyone under the sun to buy that novel are leaving the writing business in droves. The Get-By People are complaining that "sales aren't what they used to be." They're complaining that "free doesn't work anymore." They're wondering why no one is praising their (three-year-old) work.

How come these Get-By People aren't rich and famous?

Because the publishing industry does replicate the real world most of the time.

Very few Get-By writers ever have long-term success with their first novel. That's true of the past and it's true now. Remember, the traditional publishing industry works on velocity. Occasionally, a first-timer writes a kick-ass novel, and traditional publishing rewards that writer with lots of push, and a visit to the bestseller list.

Sometimes, that first-timer is a Get-By writer. The Get-By traditional writer needs to write the "sophomore" effort. The Get-By writer hasn't even started their second novel—often waiting to "see how the first one does." The Get-By writer is usually late on that second novel's deadline, and by the time the novel gets turned in, all that hype and promotion is years in the past. The second novel often fails in traditional publishing terms.

If that Get-By writer signed a three-book contract, the writer then needs to finish the third book, but never will. The publisher will cancel the contract or, when the publisher demands the book, the Get-By writer will shape up for one last effort. There will be no new contract after that third book.

In indie publishing, no one pushes the Get-By writer to write the second and third novels. Some Get-By writers realize they need to write a second book, but most never do. The Get-By writers who write that second book will rarely write a third.

By then, the Get-By writers are exhausted by their promotion efforts and all the work that writing is.

Besides, they didn't get rich quick like Amanda Hocking (not a Get-By writer), Hugh Howey (not a Get-By writer) or the half dozen other writers who rose to the notice of the traditional press as indie success stories.

The Get-By writers will move on to the next scheme, just as they move to a new job in the Real World, once their employer starts pushing them to actually do the work they're assigned.

When I quit that publishing job years ago, Editor Greg had already left to start his own business. His replacement, Young Former

Salesman Boy (younger than me—and I was twenty-four), begged me to stay.

"You're the only one who gets anything done around here," he said.

It didn't sway me.

I have no idea what happened to all of those Get-By secretaries—I mean editorial assistants—who dithered at their jobs, stretching thirty minutes of work into eight hours. I did know that Young Former Salesman Boy got Editor Greg's job because YFSB was a top salesman—which meant he had a work ethic. And I suspect that work ethic doomed those Get-By secretaries.

If you want to be a successful writer, you can skate for a year or two or even four or five. Some of those Get-By writers are fantastic storytellers. A few traditionally published Get-By writers are great wordsmiths. Their first (and if they can, second) novels do well. Readers want another book, but they don't get that next book—not from the Get-By writer.

Generally speaking, readers buy a book only once. (And often—if they use libraries or download freebies—they don't pay for a book at all.) A few readers might like a book enough to buy it for someone else. A few more readers will tell friends about the book, sparking extra sales.

But after a while, readers find other writers' books to enjoy. The Get-By writers will see their sales drop and drop and drop, and then think that no one appreciates their hard work.

But a lack of appreciation is not what happened. Readers *did* appreciate the work. They've just moved on to someone else's work.

If you want a long-term career as a writer, you can't get by. You can't tweak algorithms forever. You can't continually change your cover and blurb to convince readers you've published a new book. You can't even get by in traditional publishing, because they'll want another book.

If you're traditionally published *and* have a graduate degree you can teach. A lot of college professors dine out on that one book they published fifteen years ago. So do a lot of public speakers who go from conference to conference, rather like the one-hit wonders in music who hold concert after concert in increasingly smaller venues, playing their hit song and the ten other songs from their only album (along with a few covers).

Honestly, though, it seems to me—and remember, I'm not a get-by kinda person—that getting by is a lot more work than actually doing the work. You have to constantly figure out how to get people's attention while hiding the fact that you're not doing much. Seems like a whole lotta effort for a whole lotta nothing.

To say I'm not sympathetic is a huge understatement. I'm also not impressed. I've been known to ask aloud at jobs where I was the manager or at businesses I've owned if anyone knew whether we could actually demand that the Get-By Person we'd just gotten rid of could pay us back for all the time that person wasted.

I know that's not fair, because as the boss, I'm just as culpable for the Get-By People as the people are themselves. I hired them; I didn't see the problems fast enough; I have to deal with the leftover mess.

Just like the spouses and friends of get-by writers have to do when those writers finally give up or implode or just walk away from their dream.

Get-By People can survive in the real world by moving from job to job. But writers can't. So if you're trying to get by, ask yourself why you're even writing. If writing is your dream, then learn how to change your habits. I realize that's not an easy thing to do.

There are a million books out there on improving productivity or changing bad work habits into good ones. Buy those. Maybe take our workshop on productivity.[7] Even if you don't finish the work (and if you're a get-by person, you won't), maybe some of the questions will spark something in you and help you learn how to actually do the job.

The only way to achieve your writing dreams is to work on them—and even for those of us who don't skate through life, that work is hard.

It's also fun—and, it would seem to me, a lot more fun than just getting by.

Often, writers aren't trying to game the system. They're just trying to become more successful. There are a million writing books that tell you to do what everyone else does. Agents and traditional book editors tell you the same thing. Why? Because they believe they can sell a copy of something. They have trouble selling something new.

Fortunately, we no longer have to rely on those people. So now, it's time to listen to our mothers and stop…

CHAPTER FIVE

FOLLOWING THE CROWD

We all have those moments when we think, *Jeez, if I just write [insert latest trend here], I'll do so much better than I'm already doing.* It doesn't matter how well we're already doing. There's always a better.

If you've been in the business a long time, you have a follow-up thought: *I know how to do [latest trend]. It wouldn't take much.*

And if you were in traditional publishing, and occasionally wrote tie-ins or some novel that your traditional editor demanded you write, you have a third thought: *I've played in someone else's universe before. It wouldn't take me long to churn out something just like [latest trend].*

Yes, note that I used the phrase "churn out," which I complained about in Chapter Three. I did so deliberately. Because that's the mindset you end up in. You're not writing for the joy of the art. You're not writing what you want. You're writing what you think is required for success.

A lot of people end up with an okay short-term career doing just that—writing the latest trend, whatever it is. When that trend eases, they move onto the next trend, and the next, until they burn out. Sometimes, for some of them, following the trend works, and they find their niche. But for a lot of folks, they wake up one day to find themselves not wanting to go to their writing desk because sitting there feels too much like the day job they quit (or are still working in the hopes of a windfall).

When I say "short-term," I say it from the perspective of a long-term career. I mean a five-to-ten year career in publishing, with only two or three years of real success. It's a career. It's something to be proud of. But it isn't a lifetime career, which so many writers say they want.

I firmly believe in writing what you love. Even when I was writing tie-in fiction, I wrote what I loved. *Star Trek* and *Star Wars* got me into science fiction back when I was a kid. They had hijacked my imagination. I still adore that Classic *Star Trek* universe, and all Chris Pine's James T. Kirk showed me was that I am a super huge fan of Captain James T. Kirk, if he's written and acted properly, no matter who portrays him (Sorry, William Shatner—I like you too, but I like Kirk more).

I loved the original *Star Wars* film, loved, loved, loved *Empire Strikes Back*, and was okay with *Return of the Jedi*. Those were the only films that were out when I took on my *Star Wars* gig. Every other series I wrote in, from *Quantum Leap* to *Roswell*, I was a fan of first.

In fact, I turned down a lot of tie-in work for projects that I wasn't a fan of. And when I say a lot, I mean hundreds of thousands of dollars' worth of tie-in work.

I know I can't write well about something I don't enjoy.

I write in a lot of genres because I read a lot of genres. I write a lot of short stories for themed anthologies to stretch myself. Once in a while when I write a theme anthology story, I discover a sub-genre I don't really want to tackle again, but mostly I learn the ins and outs of the genres, and often I get too many more ideas to ever finish before I die.

Writing novels to follow a trend (even if it stretches me) is something I won't do. Novels take too much time, and you have to sink into them, or at least I do. I need to lose myself in the world that I'm writing about, and losing myself means a full commitment.

Frankly, if I want to write the latest thing, if I want to be trendy instead of artistic, I'd've taken the jobs I was offered in Hollywood, writing screenplays for television shows, and making a small fortune. I've worked collaboratively, and I've successfully written both screenplays and radio dramas. (By "successfully," I mean they were produced. I got paid for some things that weren't produced as well.) Screenplays and radio dramas are fun until they're not, and when they're not fun, they're awful.

But trend-following in novel-writing, that's generally not collaborative. That's just being outer-directed instead of inner-directed.

What do I mean by outer-directed? Someone else or something else—in this case, a trend—determines what you write from day to day. Nothing wrong with that, except…

To me—and this is probably just me—it completely defeats the point of being a freelance writer. If I wanted a day job, I'd get one. If I want someone to tell me what to do, then I'd have a boss. If I wanted to guess trends, I'd work in advertising.

I don't want to do any of that.

At heart, I'm both a rebel and an artist, and those two aspects of my personality have allowed me to freelance successfully for decades.

I know how hard it is, though, to see folks who started with you who are, in your outside opinion, doing better than you are.

In some cases, another writer actually is having more success. She is writing in the right subgenre or she's hit the cultural zeitgeist or—here's the hard one for many authors to admit—she's just a better storyteller than you are.

But if you're a long-time observer of writing careers, like I am, you realize that today's success story is tomorrow's struggling writer.

Yes, that writer's struggling from a different place—a place you might consider successful—but she's often having problems she couldn't even have imagined at the start of her career.

Those of us who went to Clarion Writers' Workshop have all experienced having someone in the class end up more success-ful than we are. In my class's case, the initial success story was a writer whose work was on the Hugo and Campbell ballot when he arrived at class. He intimidated the heck out of all of us.

When we survivors of that class got together in 2011, he said, "I often joke that my Clarion class has written a hundred novels, and Kris wrote most of them." Everyone laughed, including me, but it made me realize that somewhere along the way, I had be-come—at least to him—the success story of our Clarion class. It was a weird feeling.

It's an even weirder feeling when one of your students does better than you do at something you'd like to succeed at. A while back, a friend of mine taught at Clarion. This friend has published dozens of novels, but none have hit any bestseller lists. One of her students sold a novel right out of Clarion for five times what my friend made on any of her novels. That student became the Hot Young Thing in the front part of this decade.

Dean and I have experienced that as well. We've had students who hit the major bestseller lists with series, and those students remain on the lists. We've had students who've won all kinds of prestigious awards. We've had students crack markets I still can't crack (like *The New Yorker*).

We never take credit for our students' successes—I mean, how can I claim I'm responsible for someone repeatedly hitting

The New York Times list with a series when I've never done it? (I'm not that needy or hypocritical.) Those former students are doing something right. They're great writers who tell amazing stories—and guess what? Those former students have a fantastic work ethic (which was visible at the workshops they attended before the success hit).

I've known other writers who also teach who end up jealous of their former students or who denigrate the students' success. And that just reflects poorly on the writer-teacher. I know it's hard for some writers to watch others be successful, and I also know that *everyone* when they're starting out believes that there's a secret formula to being a successful writer.

There is: work hard, write a lot, and don't quit.

But you will *never* reach the same level of success as your friends. Their careers are *theirs*. The careers are dynamic, and as individual as your writer friends are.

Plus, all careers have ups and downs. Even the biggest bestseller struggles with *something*—maybe in the craft or maybe in the business. What every successful writer learns is that complaining about problems gets this response (often accompanied with a sneer): *I'd love to have that problem.* So the writer doesn't talk about problems anymore.

When Dean and I first met, we had several long talks about the problems of writer-couples. We knew some friends who broke up when one person in the couple became successful. (This isn't limited to writers, by the way. Sometimes couples break up when one person in the relationship makes more money or gets a better job or gets more acclaim. I think it's a sad side of human nature.)

Dean and I kept talking about this issue to make sure we were on the same page. That page was this: We'd stay together even if one of us was more successful than the other. More than that, we'd cheer each other on.

As Dean said back then, one of us will always be more successful than the other one, but over a lifetime, it might not be the same person. And that's proven to be true. Early on, Dean had more success—he'd sold a lot more fiction than I had. Then I became a critical darling (and the editor of *The Magazine of Fantasy & Science Fiction*), winning lots of awards and getting great reviews. That continued, but Dean out-earned me (by tens of thousands of dollars), and we both found that ironic.

Because early on in our relationship, he cared more about acclaim, and I cared more about making a living. Yet, the universe made sure *I* had the acclaim and *he* made a better living.

We've had all kinds of ups and downs in our careers. Then we had careers that branched out into their own smaller careers. Some of my pen names are more successful than others. (Now, that's a weird feeling: One part of me is so much more successful than another part—and they're both me!) Dean has had the same experience. And we have some interesting success as Kris&Dean (or Dean&Kris, depending on how you look at it).

Our early discussions made us hyperaware of the way that some authors surge into success and others don't. Our long-term careers have made it clear to us that success doesn't guarantee a *lifetime* of success.

We know a lot of *New York Times* bestsellers who no longer write. Some burned out, others moved to different professions, a handful can no longer sell books traditionally (!) because their numbers slid. (Those poor souls refuse to indie publish, too, and I think that's just too bad. They have fans. They can write again. They're just not willing to work outside of the traditional structure.)

I've had several long talks with a number of the latest Hot Young Things—because once upon a time, *I* was a hot young thing. I won the John W. Campbell Award for Best New Writer, which takes an uphill career trajectory in SF of less than two years. It's a rather giddy experience.

Everyone wants your fiction, everyone wants to be your friend, everyone wants to take your picture—

And then, one day, someone else becomes the Hot Young Thing, and you become an Established Pro. For a lot of writers, that shift is hard. (It's not fair to call it a transition, because it happens almost overnight.)

I really tried to warn one Hot Young Thing, because he had tied his ego into being the It Writer. I knew it would end for him, and it would end badly, and he wouldn't be prepared. One day, the publishers would want his books, and the next day, his sales figures would cease to be theoretical, and he would get (or not) get a book deal based not on being an It Writer but on a track record.

He never prepared, and the loss of his It status devastated him, like I feared it would.

Another Hot Young Thing listened when I warned her about the possible change coming up. She asked how to sustain a career, and I advised her (mostly on short fiction). She took a lot of the advice I gave her, and is considered one of the SF field's most valuable talents.

Yes, she too ceased being the It Writer, but she's still got a solid career. Because she understood career trajectories, and planned for the days beyond that early giddy success.

Why am I talking about Hot Young Things and It Writers when it comes to chasing trends? Because publishers chase trends all the time—including the hottest writer, the best genre, the perfect novel—and writers try hard to fulfill that.

Traditional book publishers, because of their business model, chase short-term trends because traditionally published books only have a short time to earn a lot of money. Traditional book publishers move from trend to trend, hot writer to hot writer, searching for what'll sell today, not yesterday.

I get it. Their business model depends on it, still.

But writers—indie and traditional—who chase trends are thinking short term.

First, a trend will have already peaked by the time you notice it.

Second, those writers who are trying to game the Amazon algorithm, to see what categories the books at the top of the charts are in, are chasing trends that might change *next week*. Unless you're writing really, really fast, or unless you're writing short stories, chasing trends using that method is an exercise in fruitlessness.

Besides, it won't pay off long term.

Trends cycle. Urban fantasy used to be called contemporary fantasy. Contemporary fantasy was hot twenty years ago, then died out, and then came back disguised as "urban." Traditionally published writers often couldn't repackage their old books (and publishers let them languish).

But now, in this new world, where writers have control, they can repackage those old books, put the proper modern label on them, and discover a whole new audience.

That's part of long-term thinking.

The true aspect of trend-following, though? The real short-term part of it? It's not the word "trend." It's the word "following."

You're always playing catch-up. You're always trying to do what someone else has already done—and, in fact, what someone else has already done better and in a fresher manner.

You're just grabbing coattails.

An agent whom I should have fired sooner than I did once complained that I always wrote in genres she had trouble selling. (Boo-hoo.) And she told me to follow trends. I told her that the best writers don't *follow* trends. The best writers *set* trends.

Something a writer wrote from his heart took off, and readers responded. They didn't respond to the plot or the identifiably different thing. They responded to the whole package—the enthusiasm of the writer (visible through the story), the storytelling, the perspective, the voice, the setting, the characters—most of which is impossible for someone else to replicate.

Because the key words here are "heart" and "enthusiasm."

J.K. Rowling wrote a book set in a magical boarding school. There was an entire tradition of British and American literature set in boarding schools. Publishers at the time thought the entire idea *passé*. That first book got rejected a lot—primarily for the fact that its idea had been done to death in British and American literature, and was no longer trendy.

But Rowling persevered, sold the first book, and the book she wrote from her heart—her passion—because she couldn't *stop* writing that book—became a worldwide phenomenon.

There are only so many worldwide phenomena, and not every writer can be one. But every writer can attract readers who like the writer for her unique perspective, voice, and storytelling ability.

When you follow, you lose that uniqueness—and quite often, you lose the passion too. That's why follower-writers burn out. Why you often hear them at writers conference, speaking with contempt about the entire creative process.

Why write when writing is drudgery?

And why follow trends these days, when indie publishing has opened the entire world for a writer?

Some of my books don't sell well in the United States, but they sell extremely well in Australia or in Europe. Some readers know me as a non-fiction writer (which still surprises the heck out of me). Some readers only know my romance name. Some readers only read certain science fiction novels, and some readers only read my mysteries.

If I limited myself to writing only the hottest, most trendy things, I'd lose readers. If I had limited myself to writing only the hottest, most trendy things before I was ever published, I would never have attracted those readers in the first place.

I worry about trend-followers, just like I worry about the latest Hot Young Thing. Because both are setting themselves up for a fall.

I truly believe that trend-followers want to be long-term writers. I believe trend-followers love writing, and see trend-following as the only way to be successful.

But success isn't an upward line on a graph. Success is a wave—sometimes you're up, and sometimes you're down. Following trends only makes that wave into a series of pyramids that don't share walls. A huge up, followed by a terrible fall. Most writers never make it to the next up after a terrible fall.

But they will have had a year or two of success.

Maybe for some people, that's all they need.

Me, I enjoy doing what I do. I have a job that I love, and I'm able to do it, because sometimes readers like what I do.

I've had bestsellers and I've had complete flops. It's great when a book sells well. It's disappointing when a book doesn't.

But the key isn't how the book *sells*. The key is the writing. I always ask myself if I accomplished the creative task I was trying when I started that book. Did I write the best book I could? Did I learn everything I could from writing that book? Now, with the benefit of hindsight, am I happy I wrote the book?

If I answered *yes* to those questions, I deem the book a success.

If readers like it, then the book is blessed.

If they didn't, then I got some practice in.

I move onto the next project—the next project I'm *passionate* about, not the next project I write to hit a trend. Because enjoying my work matters more to me than some outward measure of success.

That's the artist-rebel.

The irony is that often, enjoying my work and finding my passion leads to the success so many others chase.

To me, that's the secret of a long-term career. Stop chasing, and wander along your own path. If you do it long enough, you'll notice that some people have joined you.

And that, my friends, is completely cool.

Now that I've told you what not to do as you write, let me ex-plain what you should do. Once again, I'll use examples from the "real world," as writers call non-writing jobs. (Hmmm. Some day I should explore what that really means. Just won't do it in this book.) Employees make themselves indispensible. Writers can too.

CHAPTER SIX

INDISPENSABLE

As I'm having a fascinating spring. I'm watching two of our em-ployees make themselves indispensable.

Dean and I have owned businesses, together and separately, for decades. Not just our writing businesses, but publishing businesses, retail businesses, and a host of other businesses. When we ran Pulp-house Publishing, we had one employee who was indispensable— Debb De Noux, whom everyone knew back then as Debra Gray Cook. When she left to move to New Orleans with her future hus-band, mystery writer O'Neill De Noux, we knew we needed some-one to take her place, but there was no one who could do everything Debb did, as well as deal with me and Dean at the same time.

Because, as you've probably guessed, Dean and I are not the easiest people to deal with. Allyson Longueira at WMG Publish-ing manages us very well. Fortunately, she's not only Machiavelli reincarnated (I mean that in the best possible way), she's also bril-liant, talented—and indispensable.

We have another employee working toward indispensable, and it's marvelous to see.

It's also scary. Because, as we learned with Pulphouse, when one of the indispensable people leave the business, the business staggers for a while before recovering its footing (if it ever recovers its footing).

We've done a lot of growing up since Pulphouse, and we've learned a lot about indispensable people. I hope we're putting that learning to good use.

It took me a long time to realize that there's a huge difference between a good employee and an indispensable one. In my working life, I've been an indispensable employee twice—and once was by accident.

My accidental indispensability occurred when I worked at a Midwestern radio station. I kept getting hired as interim news director. They wanted me to be the *actual* news director, but I wanted to write and freelance. So we would go through the process of hiring someone new who would flake out (or fail) and then I would step back into the job. Two different station managers told me that they wanted me in that position, but they could never get me to give up my writing dreams.

I finally had to move to another state to get away from the lure of that job.

At most of my day jobs, I was a good employee. I showed up on time, did my work to the best of my ability, cared while I was there, and did all that I was asked to do. Sometimes the jobs were beyond me (I was truly a crap-ass secretary), but even the jobs that suited me never had my full attention.

I suspect that even if those jobs had had my full attention, I still would have been one of the rotating faces of really good employees—someone who could be relied on, but who could be replaced.

Indispensable employees make the job their own. More than that, they become part of the business in a way that would fundamentally alter the business if they left.

Since I've been ruminating on that this year in relation to the other businesses we own, I noted a thought skating across the surface of my brain: *Weird that writers can't be indispensable.*

The second or third time that thought skated by, I caught it and examined it, and realized the thought was wrong. (Which was probably why it kept cropping up: It bugged me.)

Writers can be indispensable, but in a slightly different context.

I came to this sideways, from my editing experience. When I started editing (in the deepest darkest dying days of the last century), I realized that if I wanted to put together *the* definitive volume of something—let's say horror short stories—then the volume would need certain writers.

Back then, anthologies had to sell to traditional book publishers, and they always wanted Big Names. Big Names—or Brand Names—sell books, but only in the proper context.

So anthology editors who were editing horror would always scramble to get Stephen King or Dean Koontz (or both) to headline the edition. Nowadays, anthology editors hear the same thing about urban fantasy—Laurell K. Hamilton or Jim Butcher would be dreams, along with Charlaine Harris or Patricia Briggs.

But...and here's the big thing, I mentioned doing the *definitive* anthology, and sometimes that would mean putting together a different group of writers.

When I came of age in reading, the definitive science fiction anthology had to have Isaac Asimov, not because he was a bestseller, but because he was known in the outside world as *The* Science Fiction Author.

An inside-the-field definitive anthology needed Harlan Ellison and Ursula K. Le Guin. The writers that readers *expected*. The writers whose bylines gave the anthology credibility.

Recently, Cat Rambo has been posting some ads from the early 1990s on Facebook, ads for book imprints, and back then, traditional book publishers would also line up definitive midlist writers. A traditional publishing horror line, for instance, would have no cache without John Skipp, Craig Spector, or Kathe Koja. Not bestsellers, but *the* writers of the day—the writers whose presence said *Yes, this editor, this publisher* knows *what they're doing.*

Some of that is trendiness, sure. And some of it is branding. But really, it's because those writers had a body of work that made them indispensable to their genres.

One way to identify these writers is this: If some reader in the know has to defend her reasons for *disliking* that writer, then that writer is indispensable. (If the same reader has to explain who that writer is to another in-the-know reader, then that writer is *not* indispensable. Maybe up-and-coming, but not indispensable.)

You see this less today for a variety of reasons. Because the traditional publishing industry contracted bestselleritis in the late 1990s and decided *every* book had to be a bestseller and successful midlisters needed to be jettisoned, the indispensable writers vanished. They didn't have time to build the kinds of careers that made them known for great quality, even if they never hit a bestseller list.

That was in books. You'd never see a book imprint advertise its list today, hoping that the midlist names would guarantee quality. Now those names get hidden if they're on the list at all.

From 1997 to 2009, the indispensable writer vanished from the bookstore shelves and showed up in the short fiction markets. There are writers whose work is exceedingly well known to short story readers, writers whose work is unknown to novel readers.

And this phenomenon isn't limited to one genre. The mystery magazines and mystery anthologies have their list of indispensable writers (some of whom were gracious enough to write for me in our *Fiction River Special Edition: Crime*). The science fiction magazines have their own list of indispensable writers, as does the tiny horror anthology field. There are an entire group of literary writers whose only oeuvre is short fiction. Eventually, they might get a short fiction collection—and the main difference between them and their genre counterparts is that the literary short fiction collection will be reviewed in places with larger circulations than genre publications—places like *The New Yorker* or *The Washington Post*.

So that's one traditional publishing area where writers are still indispensable. (This also happens in literary nonfiction, in long-form journalism, in tech writing, and so on. But let's just focus on fiction here.)

But my twisted analysis caught another skating thought—editors were trying to communicate quality to *readers*. Which meant that readers had already determined that these writers were indispensable.

Let me repeat: *Readers* had determined that these writers were indispensable.

In the days before algorithms and Goodreads, the only way to know what readers were thinking was through purchases, surveys, and letters to the editor. For example, when I was editing *The Magazine of Fantasy & Science Fiction*, I knew that putting certain names on the cover would make the sales go up. Yes, these names could be brand names, like Stephen King, but often they were favorites of the regular readers, writers like R. Garcia y Robertson or Esther M. Friesner.

That was a quantitative measure of a writer's power within one publication. Often we'd get letters asking when the next Friesner story would appear or if we planned to publish Richard Bowes again. We would do our best to answer with a definitive yes.

Now, those tools remain important, but so do the algorithms and online tools. If traditional publishers were smart, they would start rebuilding their midlist, using some of these tools.

In the past, readers conferred indispensability but the gate-keepers had to notice. Magazine editors noticed first. (Which was why, when I started, new book editors would come to magazine editors to find that hot new writer.) The book editors would then nurture the young writer toward indispensability.

What that meant was that a group of readers felt it *necessary* to buy that writer's next book. The key was that the group of readers had to continue to grow. Slow growth was fine, but growth was necessary.

Of course, once traditional publishing caught bestselleritis, it abandoned that thinking.

But magazine publishers never did, which is one reason that even as traditional book publishing contracted, the number of genre fiction magazines has grown dramatically in the 21st century.

Now that writers have control of their own careers, they need to understand that indispensability is within their reach. They have to grow their own readership, becoming a favorite writer of an ever-growing group of readers.

In my book *Discoverability*, I analyzed how readers approached writers. For example, everyone has a favorite writer. But that favorite writer is not the same from person to person to person. If you don't understand what I mean, check out the book or the post on readers on my website.[8]

What you want to become, as a writer, is indispensable to a group of readers. (Remember: No writer is indispensable to *every* reader.)

How do you become indispensable? That's hard to define.

But I'm going to give it a shot.

1. Don't Settle for Good. Think about this from the perspective of jobs you've held. There are dozens of very good, but forgettable employees. If necessary, they can be replaced. Good writers are the same. In every city and town, good writers are trying to break into publishing in one way or another. Either they try to get published in traditional venues or they're trying to make their way as indies. These writers have initial traction. After all, the good employee (the good writer) can become indispensable over time. But good only goes so far, because good is achievable. Moving beyond good is much, much, much harder.

2. Do *More* Than What's Expected. Good employees do their jobs. Often good employees do exactly what they're told to do and nothing more. They do that one thing very well, but that's all they do.

Same with good writers. If the current trend is vampire horses in a dystopian universe, then good writers will write a good vampire horse story with all of the "successful" elements.

That'll sell books for a while. As long as the readers want vampire horses and as long as there's a relative dearth of vampire horses, then the good writer will succeed. But when there's a glut of vampire horses and the good writer does nothing unique with those vampire horses? Then the readers will move on, and the good writer will get forgotten.

I know a lot of indie writers who are running from trend to trend to trend, trying to keep up with the readers. What good employees those writers are. They're doing the best job they can, as someone else defines the job.

The difference is that the indispensable writer is the one who defines the subgenre and the job because the indispensable writer takes the next step...

3. Put Yourself Into Your Work. Yeah, yeah, you've heard that a million times. So many writers add just a little bit, maybe setting their vampire horse novel in their own hometown or something like that.

But that's not what I mean. When I say *put yourself into your work*, I mean write something that only you could have written. So what if vampire horses are trendy? Maybe you want to write about fairy princesses, even though the trend is passé. Write it anyway. Make the readers rediscover why they once loved fairy princesses.

If you love vampire horses, then write a vampire horse novel like no other. Make it something you love rather than something you think someone else will love.

Do the work for *you*.

4. Take Risks. Season Eight of *The Voice* started this past week, and in the middle of the auditions, Pharrell Williams told a singer who didn't get picked by any of the celebrity coaches that the singer spent too much time in his own comfort zone. Good employees stay in their comfort zone. Good writers do the same.

Writers who will become indispensable some day step outside of their comfort zones all the time. That's one reason I write for a variety of short fiction anthologies. Someone gives me an assignment and I think: *I can't write that*. But I try. And I often learn something in doing so.

Or let's look at it this way. How many times have you, as a *reader*, slowly stopped reading a once-favorite author because you knew *exactly* where each novel was heading? Once upon a time, that novelist's voice was new to you, and so wherever she took you was fascinating. But after four or five books taking you on the exact same journey, maybe with different characters and a slightly different setting, you stop buying that author's work the minute it comes out.

Sure, you might read that author's work on a chocolate ice-cream night—the kind of night where you want to know exactly what you're going to get. But eventually, you even stop doing that because some other writer has stepped into the comfort position. Or worse, you forget that you used to read that writer.

Those writers are good. But they're repeating themselves. They've found a lane and a pace, and they're staying in it until someone else forces them off the road.

5. Be Willing to Fail. Good employees try not to make a mistake. They try to be perfect. But there is no such thing as perfect in real life.

There's also no such thing as perfect in writing. (See this post on my website or read about it more in depth in my book *The Pursuit of Perfection*.[9] In fact, trying to be perfect is one thing that will guarantee that you as a writer (and as a person) will get stuck in the same groove over and over again. When you take risks, you have to expect failure. The failures will be hard, but they'll be survivable.

The fascinating thing about *artists* who fail? Those failures are often among the most interesting things they do. Think of the comedians like Johnny Carson who was best when he was bombing on stage, or the singers who manage to recover in the middle of a suddenly bad performance. Sometimes a writer's failures point the way to the writer's greatest success. Sometimes that failure is a test-run for a future project. Sometimes the failure happens simply because the market wasn't ready for the innovative piece—and years later, that innovative piece gets rediscovered.

The most important thing about someone who is indispensable?

6. Always, Always, Always, Strive to Improve. Never believe you know it all. Never believe that there's nothing left for you to learn. You can always get better, always improve, always find some way to stretch yourself.

Those writers who get stuck in the perfect groove? They dig themselves in so deeply that they can't even see the rest of the road. But if you're constantly striving, you're always looking around to find out how to better your craft.

Dean recommends watching *The Voice* to the readers who follow his blog because we both learn a lot from the professional musicians who give advice. *We* learn. I'm constantly reading business books—not how-to books as much as books on the history of other businesses in the arts, to see how they survived (or didn't), how they innovated (or didn't), and how they grew (or didn't). I'm fascinated by that stuff, and I'm constantly learning.

I realized this past Sunday as I watched the Academy Awards that I'd been so busy building all these businesses, I had closed down a major source of creative learning for me. I had stopped seeing first-run films. I need to find time to watch movies again, because that form of storytelling often advances my own.

Finally...

7. Be the Best at What You Do—However You Define It. That almost sounds contradictory to "keep learning," but it's not. Because being the best is a constantly moving target. There's always someone better waiting in the wings, someone who learned from you, someone who has found a way to build a better mousetrap.

Take that design and make it your own. Keep striving to be the best. You might never achieve it (at least in others' eyes) but work for it in your own.

Bottom line: Writing is not a competition. We are not fighting each other for readers. Every reader can read more than we'll ever be able to write.

We're actually working day in and day out to leave a body of work behind. I mentioned some names above who were considered the heart and soul of a genre twenty years ago. In the case of the horror genre, the genre vanished, and those writers could have vanished with the genre.

They didn't. Because they all had other interests and other strengths and, at their core, they didn't define themselves as horror writers. They called themselves *writers*, and they were constantly working to improve, constantly striving to be the best *writers* they could be.

Sometimes you're the hot new thing and sometimes you're the voice of a genre and sometimes you're someone's favorite writer. Those things aren't mutually exclusive, but they don't always happen at once—and most importantly, they don't stay constant.

If I asked you who your favorite writers are now, you'd give me a list. But I can guarantee you that if I had asked you the same question when you were fifteen, you would have given me a very different list. And twenty years from now, you'll give me yet another list.

Some names might remain the same. (Stephen King has stayed on my list since I was a teenager.) But more often than not, the names are constantly evolving. My indispensable writers are constantly changing, as more and more writers come into my consciousness.

I'm sure that's the same for you.

You can't force someone to like you. You can't force someone to like your writing either.

But you can do the very best job you possibly can, take risks, occasionally fail, and strive to be better each and every day.

And if you do those things, you'll become an indispensable writer for a group of readers. If you *continue* to do those things, you'll become an indispensable writer for a growing group of readers.

Never aspire to good. Because you'll end up at good enough.

Aspire to be the best.

Grow and learn. And keep writing. Each and every day.

Now that you've become indispensable, you have it made, right? Time to rest on those laurels and enjoy the fruits of your labors.

Not so fast. I'm speaking to all of you, of course, but primarily to those of you for whom success came quickly. You have some rough times ahead. You just might not know it yet. Or you might be getting an inkling. Or maybe you think your luck just ran out.

Naw. Those of you with early success had beginner's luck. And believe me, you can survive it. This chapter will tell you how.

CHAPTER SEVEN

BEGINNER'S LUCK

One of the most astonishing moments I had as the editor of *The Magazine of Fantasy & Science Fiction* occurred at the Hugo Awards ceremony. A writer won a Hugo with a short story I had rejected. He got in my face—literally inches away from me—and said,

"I bet you're sorry you rejected me, aren't you?"

Then he bounced away from me before I had a chance to answer him. How would I have answered him?

I would have said, "Congratulations on your win," and I would have meant it.

But had he obnoxiously pressed the point, I would have added, "I still don't like your story."

Editing is about taste. We reinforce that lesson every year at our anthology workshop. The writing quality in the workshop is incredibly high. We open the workshop to professional writers only—folks who've published a lot, whether fiction or nonfiction, indie or traditional. Some writers come back every year, partly to test their abilities to write six stories to order in six weeks, partly to see old friends, and partly to see the editors bicker.

And the editors do bicker. A *lot*.

Mostly, we bicker over our points of view. What happens is this: Generally one of us will think Story A is brilliant, and some other editor will think it tragically flawed. We're editors and writers and opinionated as hell, so we argue our positions. But we respect each other, and we know that some of us have an affinity for stories that the rest of us don't like.

When it comes down to choosing between two stories that are not to our taste, we six editors have learned to rely on each other.

In fact, we always agree on one thing: The editor who purchases the story is the final judge of its quality. That editor has to love the story to buy it.

I'm sure the editor who bought that Hugo-winner loved the story. I didn't. But even then, I knew that editing was about taste.

The writer didn't.

He also thought his shit didn't stink.

Is he still writing? I don't know. Is he still publishing? I don't know. But I do know this: He's not being published in science fiction. In fact, in science fiction, his career didn't last beyond a few years of short stories. (I'm not sure if there was a novel or not; I didn't pay attention.)

Over the years, I've run into a lot of writers like this guy. One of those writers wrote one of most unintentionally funny letters I'd ever read to Dean. As editor of *Pulphouse: A Fiction Magazine*, Dean had rejected one of the writer's short stories. The writer wrote back to say that he had just sold his first novel and that Dean didn't recognize the quality of this writer's work. In fact, the writer added, Dean should eat that writer's manuscript for the "only words of substance" Dean would ever have inside him.

I do remember that writer's name because Dean tells that story with great delight (as an example of writer ego/idiocy). The writer's book appeared and vanished that year with no follow-up. I just Googled the writer's name, and discovered that for about two years, he self-published a few other short stories. Nothing since 2012, though, which does not surprise me.

Why doesn't it surprise me? Because I think this guy is a bad writer? He's not. He's eloquent, particularly when he's pissed off. But his I'm-better-than-anyone-else attitude ensured that he will never have a long-term career in the arts.

There are all kinds of egotistical writers. You find them at every writers' conference or on every writers' online forum. One book sale to New York, one major traditional honor, and the writers will believe they're better than every other writer.

But there's a new twist to the old breed. It's an indie twist. I've seen it at some conferences and workshops in the past few years. It's the indie writer who, after receiving constructive advice *which the writer asked for*, dismisses that advice by saying, "Well, I sell thousands of books per month."

The writer usually *is* selling thousands of books per month. Obviously, the writer is doing something very, very right. Readers like the books and buy more.

When such writers come to me for advice on craft, I always think they're asking about *future* projects, what they can do to *improve* their craft. When I tell them what I think they need to work on (remember, the advice was solicited), they respond with that sales thing.

So why did they come to me if they're already doing well? These writers come to me (and others with traditional publishing experience) to be validated. They want us to tell them how very brilliant they are. In fact, they want us to understand that brilliance can happen outside of the traditional framework.

I know it can. I read a lot of writers who are indie published. I love their work. I watch a lot of my friends do exceptionally well with sales, often at thousands per month, while publishing their own books.

Those writers continue to learn. In fact, several of them came to the anthology workshop (and have come to past workshops). I've seen these indie writers continue to grow in ability each and every year. These writers are *improving*. They're augmenting what they do well, and working hard to improve their weaknesses.

They're succeeding.

If I already know that writers can have thousands of sales per month outside of the traditional framework, why do I say that the writers who ask for advice and then dismiss it with their sales figures are like the guy who wanted me to admit I was wrong when I rejected his one short story?

Because—honestly—I worry about those indie writers who only cite their sales numbers. All writers can improve, even those of us who've been in the business for thirty years.

Generally speaking, writers who have such great sales figures early on have one skill that's very hard to teach. They know how to tell a good story. Even if there are other problems in the writing—clichéd characters, non-existent setting, poor grammar—the writer's superior storytelling skills shine through.

It's almost like looking through a dirty window at a badly decorated house. Yes, you'll be comfortable there, but the house could use a good cleaning, some paint, and new furniture. If the home owner made those improvements, the house wouldn't be a good house: It would be the best house in town.

Here's the attitude that those writers—from the award-winner to the word-eater to the sales-figure folks—don't have. They don't understand that if they want to grow as writers, they need to look at those awards, traditional book sales, or high volume of indie book sales as a *starting* platform, and improve from there.

John Grisham did that. He felt like he had a lot to learn as a writer, even as *The Firm* hit every bestseller list in the world, and he set out to learn even more. His craft has improved tremendously. His latest novels are *amazing*. His short stories are breathtaking.

Yes, the storytelling chops are still there, but they're even stronger. Grisham always had a can't-put-it-down quality, but the books were "thin" and not always memorable. Now, the books are not only memorable, but achingly so. Look at the storytelling chops from *A Time To Kill* (his first written novel) to *Sycamore Row* (using the same characters). In *A Time To Kill*, you can see the furniture move as Grisham sets the bits of his plot into motion.

In *Sycamore Row*, the furniture is part of the story, and when the furniture moves, we don't see it until the author wants us to. A completely different level of skill. Both books are readable, but one is masterful—and it ain't the first one.

J.K. Rowling also grew as a writer after her first novel sale. The first chapter of *Harry Potter and The Sorcerer's (Philosopher's) Stone* has no setting except a cupboard and a street (and maybe a street lamp). Look it up if you don't believe me.

She continued to learn her craft even though she had already sold *millions* of copies of her books.

Looking back over what I just wrote, I realize you might misunderstand what I mean by the writers' attitudes. Do I mean that because writers diss gatekeepers, the writers will fail?

Not at all.

I mean that writers who believe that one publication, one award, or some other kind of early success means that they're God's Gift to Literature will always vanish.

Early success is a minefield. I write this as someone who had a lot of early success. I won the John W. Campbell Award for Best

New Writer in 1990. That's hard to do, not because of the talent involved, but because a writer has to be *noticed* in a two-year time frame to win that award. My rise as an SF short story writer was meteoric as are the careers of most Campbell winners.

Unlike many of them, though, I survived that early success. So I'm speaking from experience here when I talk about the perils of early success. I've watched more writers who had success right off the bat vanish than writers who struggled for years to achieve success.

Like the beginners who win a lot of money at a poker table or hit a home run their first time at bat, writers have beginner's luck as well. And it can be just as harmful.

These writers end up believing that writing is easy, and learning business is unnecessary. Writing *is* easy compared to, say, fighting fires or a myriad of other jobs that require dedication, intelligence, and courage. But continually telling stories and going back to the desk each and every day can be difficult.

And not everything a writer writes—I don't care who he is— will work. Sometimes a writer has to try again and again before a story bends to his will.

I've written a lot about the way that a lack of business knowledge can ruin a writing career. Quite frankly, the writers who get destroyed fastest from a lack of business knowledge are the God's-Gift writers.

Or it used to be that way.

Indie publishing has allowed a lot of business-minded people to enter the publishing industry in a way that traditional publishing discouraged. I suspect these folks will make it through the business ups and downs.

But there's a craft up-and-down cycle as well that will eventually trip these writers up, and they won't know why.

Readers tire of the same thing from the same writer over and over again. I know, I know. A bunch of you are getting ready to tell me that your favorite writer tells the same story over and over again, and you're not tired of it.

And I'll bet you cash money that writer continues to study his craft and strives to improve.

There's a career arc for writers who don't improve their storytelling skills. They publish many good-enough books in a few years (fewer years now than before, thanks to the shorter publication time for indie books). As I mentioned in Chapter Six, after a while, the readers can see everything that the writer does, and after starting a novel, will see *exactly* how that book will end. (Or, worse, the ending will come out of left field with no warning, pissing the reader off.)

Once a reader figures out everything in a writer's bag of tricks, the reader will move on to other writers, often without thinking about it. The reader might buy a few more of the writer's novels, but will eventually realize he's not reading those novels. The sales will taper off, even of the new work.

And the writer will have no idea why.

Careers in the arts are cyclical. Writers are popular for a while. Then they're less popular. Trends are hot for a few years, and then they are out-of-date and considered stale.

Genres rise in popularity, and then the popularity falls.

Now that traditional publishing has less involvement in trend-making and genre popularity, I suspect that the downs won't be troughs.

What I mean by that is this: Once a genre becomes popular, it will gain more readers. When the popularity drops off, some of those new readers will remain. So the low part of the cycle will be higher than a previous low part of the cycle.

(In the past, traditional publishing just plain old stopped publishing the "unpopular" genre except for a few bestsellers, guaranteeing that the genre would die off. Right now, trad pub is trying to do that to urban fantasy. More and more writers tell me that they can't sell the next book in their series or a book in their new UF series because trad pub says "urban fantasy doesn't sell." Yet indie writers are seeing urban fantasy sales grow.

(What trad pub is saying is that UF doesn't sell at blockbuster levels anymore, so trad pub is no longer interested. Indie is picking up the slack, and UF indie writers are doing very well indeed.)

The cyclical nature of the arts isn't just in business and genre, but also in interest over a writer. A new writer has a brand-new, never-before-heard voice, and readers flock to that. Once the voice becomes familiar, some readers will abandon that voice for other new voices.

Surviving that familiarity trap requires more than writing the same old thing. It requires the writer to step up his game.

And the God's-Gift writers don't believe they need to step up their game. After all, they've been winning. They're like the poker players who watch poker on TV, sit at a table, and make thousands of dollars during their first week.

Poker is a game of skill, as I've learned watching the career of my professional-poker-player husband. Like any game, there is chance involved, but the true professionals mitigate the luck factor and try to take it out of the equation as much as possible.

Beginners who don't understand much more than what hand of cards defeats another rely on the luck factor.

And we all know—every single one of us—that luck runs out.

God's-Gift writers are often lucky bastards, with the right book at the right time. Or with a competent short story on a topic that excites readers. Or with a series of indie books with a compelling narrative told by someone with enough skill to hold the reader's attention—for now.

But what keeps a writer in the game over the long haul—what keeps *an artist* in the game over the long haul—is a genuine humbleness combined with a willingness to learn.

This very idea actually showed up on *The Voice* last week, when one of the contestants said there wasn't a song he couldn't sing. He told this to Pharrell Williams and Lionel Richie (!). Both Richie and Williams jumped on the young man, telling him that he had to be humble.[10]

Lionel Richie took it one step further, saying, "If you're great, let [the audience] tell you. Never tell them."[11]

Richie seems to live this philosophy. In video that accompanies his album *Tuskegee*, he talks about all he learned from re-imagining his hit pop songs as country songs and singing those old hits as duets with country artists, some of whom had not been born when the hits came out.[12]

It takes courage—creative courage—to reinvent your hits. So many professional musicians of Richie's age tour the casino circuit, playing the same old tired renditions of their past glories. Richie not only reinvented his, but he also learned from artists younger than he is.

Let's focus on Richie's words. What happens when the audience tells you that you're great? Are you done? Can you rest on your laurels?

So many writers, so many artists, do. They've climbed the mountain. They've achieved greatness.

The problem is, that greatness is fleeting.

Enjoy it when it happens, but realize that ten years from now, the Hugo win or the megaselling pop hit will seem dated to a new generation.

Do you need to reinvent yourself?

No, but you do need to look at your craft—continually—and figure out ways to grow. That way, you don't get left behind as tastes change. You don't become Whatever-Happened-To or Didn't-She-Write-a-Book-Once or (God forbid) Who?-*I've*-Never-Heard-of-Her.

You'll never appeal to all readers all the time. And, quite honestly, even when you're at your most popular, not every reader will have heard of you.

Appealing to everyone should never be your goal.

Your goal should be to become the best writer *you* can be. And this year's best-writer-you should be better than last-year's-best-writer-you but not as good as next-year's-best-writer-you, because, in theory, you should keep learning and improving.

Does that mean you should take classes or go to workshops, hire editors or get a million critiques? Not necessarily. You need to figure out what works for you, and how you learn. Critiques are often destructive to writers, especially peer critiques between beginners or with professors who don't make their living as writers.

In fact, on *The Voice*, the superstar musicians often talk to the contestants about unlearning everything they picked up in their graduate music studies. If you watch, look at the sadness on the faces of the coaches when they realize someone has (or is about to) graduate from a major music school. Often as not, those artists never make it past the third round, because they're too technically perfect and their work lacks heart and emotion.

I learn a lot from artists in other disciplines, like music. I've learned a lot as I watched Lionel Richie explore the roots of his own music. I learn from artists like The Roots, who seem to know every genre of music and play them all well.

I ask a lot of questions, and when I don't know the answer, I go to someone who does. I also have a lot of students because students are always asking new questions, questions I've never considered. If I've never considered it, then I haven't learned it yet.

I watch things like *The Voice*. I read all the time. I listen to the new writers coming in, and watch what's working for them. I still read for enjoyment. I follow trends and I stretch my craft, trying things and sometimes failing spectacularly.

One of the things I do, as a series editor for *Fiction River*, is read a lot of stories in genres I'm not personally fond of. When Dean and I decided to return to editing short fiction, we decided ours wouldn't be the only voices in *Fiction River*.

We have a lot of different guest editors on different volumes. Those editors provide different voices and points of view. They often have very different taste than I do, and sometimes buy stories I don't like. I think that's a good thing—not just for *Fiction River*, but also for me.

Because those stories are in *Fiction River* and because I line edit each volume (for clarity only), I have to go deep into stories I would never normally read. I learn a lot about other forms of storytelling, about plot, about craft.

I also learn from the way that the other editors work.

I also know my limitations. Every now and then, as the supremely confused line editor, I send a story back to the volume's editor, saying the story makes no sense to me and here's why. I ask the editor to have the writer make a few revisions. Sometimes the editor says the story is fine and I'm clueless. Sometimes the editor asks for tweaks from the author that I would never think of in a million years because I don't "get" the story. I learn from both of those instances.

Sometimes I think *Fiction River* is one of the best things I've ever done for my writing.

I learn from doing. It's taken me years to find new ways to learn. I'm sure five years from now, I'll find yet another way of improving my craft.

The key, though, is that I'll still be looking five years from now.

I am not yet the best writer I can be. I'm not sure I'll *ever* be the best writer I can be.

But no matter how many awards I win, how many books I publish, or how many copies of those books I sell, I will always know I have a lot to learn as a writer.

Chasing excellence—and knowing it is ever elusive—keeps me in my writing chair. I seriously can't imagine playing the same old hits to ever-smaller audiences. I would much rather try something new and fail spectacularly, than receive applause for something I did twenty years ago.

Sometimes you've done nothing wrong as a writer, and yet ev-
erything crumbles around you. Getting through the day becomes
the definition of survival.

Once you make it through that crisis, you need to get back to
work. But how? It requires some acceptance of your new situation,
and a shift in...you guessed it...attitude.

Here's some advice on the subject that I wrote in April 2012, as
I was just coming out of one of those horrible life events.

CHAPTER EIGHT

ONE PHONE CALL FROM OUR KNEES

In 2009, Mat Kearney came out with a song called "Closer to Love,"
which is, apparently, a favorite of the DJs on the station I listen to. It
still plays in rather heavy rotation for an older song, and I hear it at
least once a week. The song isn't one of my favorites, but it has a line
that stops me every time I hear it, because it's so true.

We are, as Kearney states, just a phone call from our knees.

Dean and I have had those calls throughout our lives together—when my father died, when Dean's stepfather died. The calls
that just take your everyday life and turn it into a completely new
life, one that changes things so utterly, you can barely remember
what life was like before that moment.

We had one in August. Our friend Bill Trojan had died, leaving Dean as the executor of an estate so messy that a lawyer friend
of mine (who handles estates) called it one of the top ten estate
stories of all time. My friend did not mean that in a good way.

Our lives changed in that moment and, I swear, almost cost Dean his life one night. He blogged about this after the estate closed in February.[13] Even though his blog is extremely clear, it doesn't quite convey the pressures of living in this high-stress environment for months on end.

And that comes after years of dealing with changes in our profession, some of which we've only begun to understand in hindsight. It comes on the heels of some difficult changes in our personal life, which I'm not going to go into here. We went from high stress to high stress for almost a decade, and then, just as it seemed the stress would ease, Bill died, and we realized that we had no idea what stress was.

I'm not writing about this to complain. We're both honored by our friend's trust in us, and we're trying to do our best by him. We both miss him every day that we go without a curmudgeonly phone call, filled with both complaints, laughter, and trenchant observations about the world.

It is simply an acknowledgement of the fact that Bill's death not only caused a disruption in our day-to-day lives, tore up our hearts, and changed how we live, but it also had an impact on our writing.

Professional writers who've been to our Oregon workshops—the Master Class in particular—call these events "life rolls." When we taught the Master Class, we (along with Loren Coleman) invented a role-playing game that mimicked the way a long-time professional writer's career works. Before I go any farther, no, we're not teaching that version of the Master Class any longer, because publishing changed. We do have another version, which you can find if you go to wmgpublishingworkshops.com.

Back to the role-playing game, which we called (unoriginally) the Game, we had disruptive events coincide with every writer's role-played career. Those events were called "life rolls."

Sometimes they were positive—for example, you got married (of course, you'd lose money for the cost of the wedding plus weeks [maybe months] of work, but you might not have to pay all the bills on your own anymore). More often than not, the rolls were disruptive. We took one bestselling writer (in the Game) out for five years with a succession of life rolls that prevented her from working.

For years after the Game's invention, our students would send us personal experiences and add, "This belongs in the Game as a life roll."

Yep. Bill's death belongs in the Game as a life roll.

In order to deal with this monster estate in a timely way—a way that wouldn't permanently eat up what little funds Bill had left and our own savings—Dean let almost everything else go. He tried to write in September and somehow managed to finish some really good stories, but as October and November came along, he simply couldn't concentrate any longer—at least, not on something like writing.

He is only now turning his attention back to writing, eight months after we got that knee-dropping phone call. And I'm pleased he's doing so. I also understand the struggle. When my dad died, I couldn't read or write for six months (which plunged me into a living hell, because everything I do involves reading and writing). The counselor I was seeing at the time told me such reactions are normal, and it would ease, but in the middle of it all, it seems like there is no way out.

When we realized how hard it would be to deal with Bill's estate, we agreed that one of us had to keep our day jobs, which meant that I had to keep writing rather than go to Eugene every week with Dean to clean up the mess that Bill had left behind.

I finished a novel, continued to write my nonfiction blog, wrote some other nonfiction, and finished three novellas. The novel and the novellas were real struggles, which I blamed on the projects themselves. The nonfiction wasn't as hard, partly because I used to work in radio on a daily (sometimes hourly) deadline, and I'd trained myself to write fact and opinion under the most difficult of circumstances.

I started the next novel on the schedule and wrote, and wrote, and wrote, and wrote, and wrote, never feeling like I was getting traction, always feeling confused and out of sorts. I wasn't finishing anything, even though I produced my daily word count plus, and I'd often have to review what I wrote just to remember where I was.

The year from hell continued, with lots of other disruptions, so that we got to the point where we actually hated to hear the phone ring in the hours before we got up. (People who don't know us call before noon; our friends call at that time only in an emergency.) I keep track of what happens during the day in my desk calendar, and not a week went by without me losing an entire workday to an emergency of one sort or another. Yet I persevered, continuing work on the never-ending novel, taking time to write a short story or two under deadline, and the blog as well.

Until earlier this week, when I swear that my brain melted. I looked at the book and realized I had 100,000 out-of-order words with no real hope of figuring out what I was doing or where I was.

I talked to Dean about it, and he finally convinced me to let him help. He would read the book and see if he could find the common thread or if I had written past my ending or if I even had a book at all.

I told him I had no idea why this book wasn't working and why, even though I was writing, I couldn't seem to wrap my brain around what was happening.

He smiled at me. He then gently reminded me that we'd had a heck of a life roll in the fall.

I shook my head. He had the life roll. Look at that blog post of his: He went through a lot. I stayed home and worked.

"Sometimes," he said, "being the support staff is harder."

I disagreed then, and I disagree now. I've never seen a man work that hard in my life. That hard or that long or with that much focus. I was, and am, impressed.

Yet I know he was right about being support staff. My brain was busy these past eight months with Real Life. Imaginary worlds just weren't as vivid or as important as they usually were—and that included other people's books, television, and movies. I had little patience for anything that didn't grab my attention immediately.

I had an unacknowledged life roll.

And I had to acknowledge it—not just acknowledge it, but also acknowledge that for me, at least, it still continues. In the past two months, two more friends have died and so has my uncle. The friends, while not close friends, were still people I enjoyed and who passed away too soon (one at fifty, the other at sixty-two). My uncle, whom I hadn't spent a lot of time with since I moved to Oregon, was an influential person in my childhood, and so losing him was, in a sense, the reminder of the loss of an era.

Plus the deaths resonated with Bill's, and with my thoughts of late. Dean and I are putting our own estate in order.

The brain is starting to come back. And as it has, I realized I haven't written about life rolls in quite this way. I wrote about setbacks in *The Freelancer's Survival Guide*, but because I was dealing in general with freelancers, I didn't talk about the way life rolls can impact writing.

And they do. Because like it or not, life rolls mess with our brains, our creativity, our energy, and our ability to concentrate.

I know this. I've known it for a long time. I have taught professional writers about this for more than ten years now.

In fact, I've just watched another friend go through this same kind of slog during the same period. Her father died a few days before Bill, and she had a novel due (and a real day job). She did her best, was just a little late, and only recently mentioned that writing feels fun again.

I reminded her about life rolls.

Pot, meet kettle. Kettle, pot.

The fact is that no one does a job at 100% when something major is happening in life. We all lose focus and concentration. Some places offer family leave or compassionate time. Others put employees on reduced duties or take the employees off the complicated problems and put someone else on that job.

It's just, as writers, we don't have the luxury of putting someone else on the task. We either delay the deadline, slog through, or abandon the project altogether.

In the middle of this mess, a book dealer told me about Tony Hillerman's first missed deadline, which occurred when Hillerman's brother died, and Hillerman became executor of the estate. Hillerman had a long career and, from what the dealer told me, this happened in the middle of it. I'm sure the dealer—who is a good friend—was offering a sideways life lesson that I was ignoring.

I did my job. I finished my deadlines—except the one, the 100,000-word novel that needs an editorial eye, which it's getting at the moment. I've kept my editor at the traditional publishing house informed as to what's going on, and he's understanding.

I'm not. I want to be robo-writer, the person who can write through anything. But I don't know any writers like that. That's why we included life rolls in the Game.

Some things just slow you down or take you out for a while. And while I understand that, I sure as hell don't like it.

The thing is: I'm not sure if that 100,000-word novel would have been a mess even without the life roll. Every now and then,

I take on a project that's a stretch. Or sometimes it's even be-yond my current skill set. And I do that with or without a life roll. Those projects get tossed and restarted, redrafted usually, because I told the story in the wrong order or from the wrong character's point of view, or I wrote until I figured out what the story was, and then I had to actually write *that* story, not the story about writing the story.

In other words, even when life is normal, my process is a messy one.

It all goes back to something Neil Gaiman said once. He said that something you write with a headache is as good as something you write when you're feeling fine. *And it shouldn't be.*

But it is.

So as messy as my life has been these past few months, as hard as it's been to concentrate, I'm probably putting out the same ratio of good to bad stuff that I always do. It just *feels* worse than it is.

The key is something I tell my students: You have to give yourself a break. You must look at your work as if you still had a day job. If you'd call in sick to a real job, then don't write today. If your boss would tell you that you're being ineffectual and you need some time off so *go home, dammit*, then you should really knock off writing for the day. If you'd take a vacation or compas-sionate leave or family time at the day job, then do so as a writer.

Oh, that advice is so easy to give. So hard to take.

Dean told me two weeks ago, as more stuff happened in our lovely little spate of life rolls, that I should take April off. Instead, I've written my usual number of words of fiction, my weekly blog, and a few other nonfiction pieces. I've also started the major re-search on an estate article.

I didn't want to take April off. But I did want to quit focus-ing on the Impossible Book. So I started a project just for me, something fun. And I've knocked off early more nights than not.

I'm actually caught up on my television viewing for the first time in years. I've read two novels on the day they arrived in the mail, something I haven't done in longer than I care to think about.

And I'm starting to noodle the idea of a vacation. Somewhere easy. Somewhere close. Somewhere fun.

Life rolls knock all of us to our knees, whether the rolls come by telephone or via e-mail or by a simple knock on the door. We'll all spend some time on that floor wondering how the hell we got there.

The key is not that we've fallen, not even how long we remain on our knees with our hands hiding our faces, but how many times we're willing to get up. Once we get up again, then we go forward in the new reality, forging a new path.

My students have heard me say that countless times, and I've spoken from experience. But it doesn't matter how many times I've said it or how many times I've lived it: I still need someone else to remind me about how difficult life rolls are and how different we are after we've recovered from them.

Don't hear me wrong: I'm not giving anyone an excuse to skip writing. I'm telling you to evaluate your life and realize that at times, the writing will be hard, the business will be hard, *life* will be hard.

All we can do is get through that, and then go back to what we love.

Sometimes the key to surviving a life roll is to just get through it.

I hope I will do so with the same grace under pressure that Dean has shown these past eight months. He's been amazing. In fact, when that knee-knocking phone call came last August—and it was a phone call—I'm not even sure Dean went down. He just started moving forward with great purpose and a built-in recognition that everything had changed.

Apparently it takes me longer.

I guess it's time to deal with the fact that I've had a life roll. Now I need to deal with the fallout from it.

Time to stand up and face the music.

I just hope the music isn't a three-year-old Mat Kearney song with a devastating lyric. I'd like to listen to something else for a while.

Sometimes the troubles you have in your writing come not from tragedies or "life rolls," but from the opinions of others. Throughout the history of literature, writers have fought about the most amazing (and sometimes silly) things. But those fights get internalized, and can cause a single writer a lot of grief.

This post comes from March 2015, just before the fight I mentioned made it into the international news media. I'm not rehashing the fight here. I hope, by the time you read this, that it'll be ancient history, but it did give me a chance to examine the impact of writer wars on the writers themselves.

CHAPTER NINE

CONTROLLING THE CREATIVES

Right now, a visible group of people in the field of science fiction are engaged in a protracted battle about the genre's future. Both sides are practicing a nasty, destructive campaign against the other, and not worrying about the collateral damage they're causing on the sidelines.

Those of us who've been in the field a long time have pretty much abstained from the arguments. Not because we lack opinions. We have opinions and have discussed them with each other privately, but we remain quiet because we've seen such protracted battles before.

When I came into the field in the 1980s, I watched the remnants of two such protracted battles. The first was about the legitimacy of *Star Wars* and *Star Trek* and whether or not *Trek* and

SW fans even belonged in the genre, let alone any writers who admitted they enjoyed those things.

That first argument spilled into a sillier side argument about whether or not tie-in writers tainted their writing skills by writing novels in someone else's universe. Hugo Award winner Timothy Zahn pretty much destroyed the naysayers by writing excellent SF novels under the *Star Wars* label *and* making a small fortune doing so.

The second argument was about whether fantasy was a legitimate genre. The writer-critics agreed that *slipstream* fantasy—the kind that where you can't tell if the fantasy is something that really happened to the character or something that he misinterpreted—was legitimate. But the rest of it? That could've been crap, as judged by the terms the writer-critics used, like "fat fantasy novels," as if they were all the same, or "elfy-welfy" novels that obviously weren't up to any kind of quality whatsoever.

When I published my first novel, a not-quite-fat fantasy novel set in a magical kingdom, a writer-friend told me that I had just ruined the career I was building because I was writing crap fantasy, not real literature. He didn't receive a new asshole, but only because I was little more circumspect in those days. Now, I'd simply tell him in no uncertain terms to mind his own damn business and to let the readers decide.

If you think these kinds of arguments only occur in the SF genre, think again. In the past few years, I participated in a few group projects in the romance genre. In two cases, one of the participants was a male romance writer, and I'll be honest: Until this SF argument started, I had never before seen such naked bigotry among writers.

Some of the female romance writers *hated* that a man was involved, wouldn't admit that he could contribute anything of value, and essentially treated him (if they spoke to him at all) as if he were an imbecile. These women, all of a certain age, had had the same experience themselves in reverse in their real-world careers, so I was stunned that they would turn on a fellow human being like that, but turn they did.

The mystery field has its issues as well. Some of the issues also concern gender: There's a well-known editor in the field who has said that both women and cats have no place in mystery. I'm convinced he does this to provoke, since he's supported women in many ways (including in my own career). I have no idea what he's done for cats.

But there's also another division in mystery that runs really deep: There are mystery writers who consider those who write cozies (y'know, like the stuff Agatha Christie wrote) to be an inferior part of the genre, if part of the genre at all. On the other side, there are cozy writers who believe that the hard-boiled writers (like Raymond Chandler) destroyed a decorous genre with unnecessary violence.

While these distinctions might sound silly to the casual reader, they're extremely destructive to writers inside the various genres. I know of writers who stopped producing in the genres they loved because of the vicious attacks from one side or another. I also know of writers whose outspoken nastiness destroyed their careers with the very editors (and readers) they wanted to sell books to.

Since the advent of indie publishing, it's not as easy to destroy a career as it was in the past. An editor might not want to take a toxic writer into the fold, but the writer can self-publish. You'd think that would solve the issues of divisiveness—if writers want to write something, they can—but it hasn't. If anything, the problem has grown more pervasive, louder, and uglier.

Personally, I believe that a writer's politics and religious beliefs (including beliefs about a favorite genre) should remain off social media if at all possible, and that arguments in favor of one thing or another should be made in person, if at all.

I think it's more important to incorporate your worldview into what you write and let the readers decide whether or not they want to read your work than it is to win an argument that will seem quaint fifteen years from now. Of course, I also believe that we should all look at the way people live their lives rather than focusing on the words they use or the color of their skin.

Yeah, idealist here. One whose perfect world matches the one Dr. Martin Luther King outlined in 1963, when he said that human beings should be judged by the content of their character, not the color of the skin (or their gender or their sexual preference or—you know, all of that).

If you want to change the world, work to effect change politically or economically or through a charity. Volunteer, vote, run for office, do something active rather than try to destroy people who disagree with you. If nothing else, write fiction with the passion that you're currently investing in online flame wars and trolling.

Screaming at an enemy, with a side dish of name-calling, only leads to trench warfare. It also has an impact on some readers. I know of readers who stopped reading favorite writers because of the Hachette-Amazon dispute last summer, and I'm sure this major fight in SF is causing readers to quietly drop writers from their reading lists.

My tenure in the publishing industry has shown me that these bitter disputes are really about change. One side resists the change while the other side advocates for it, and they remain locked at each other's throats, calling each other names. The thing is, while they're screaming at each other, other writers are quietly effecting change by doing what they do best—writing fiction.

The problem for writers, particularly beginning writers, is that they hear these arguments and get indoctrinated with "shoulds."

If I had listened to that writer-friend twenty-four years ago, I would never have written The Fey series, my Kristine Grayson novels would not exist, and I would have essentially cut off a huge part of my creativity.

If I had not withstood the tie-in arguments, I would never have written some *Star Trek* novels that I'm very proud of or got to play in the *Star Wars* universe—something I had dreamed about since I was sixteen years old.

I would have let other people's opinions destroy things I love.

The problem with *all* of these arguments, from the cozy versus the hard-boiled, the fantasy versus science fiction, the women versus men, the white folks versus people of color, is that they *prescribe* how a *story* should be written.

What's wrong with writing a story from your own heritage? If the story's from a perspective that hasn't seen a lot of print, then write it. If the story's been done before (as is the case with so much white American-European fiction), write it anyway.

Write it. Because it comes from *your* personality, *your* knowledge, and *your* heritage. That story will contain your passion. Write it and let it find its audience.

I know that a lot of curated fiction—stuff that came out of traditional publishing—closed and barricaded the door to people of color (in almost all genres), to women (in most genres), and to men (in the romance genre). I know that these issues still need resolution.

I also know that indie publishing has allowed these voices to finally be heard.

That's change, and so many people are so terrified of change that they react with startling bigotry and language or behavior that they would never use in polite company. Social media has allowed a lot of horrid things to slip through the cracks—racist, discriminatory, biased, and just plain ugly stuff.

And because of it, so many newer writers are backing away from topics that they could easily write about now that the gate-keepers have lost their hold on the entry points into various fields. These newer writers are letting the opinions of others—others who, in the scheme of things really don't matter much—shut down the creative process.

What these newer writers don't realize is that a lot of these arguments are a last-ditch effort to control the conversation—and more importantly, to control the creatives.

In the past, traditional publishing controlled the creatives by keeping the doors locked to anything other than Our Kind's point of view. It didn't always succeed. Women have always had a major influence on science fiction and fantasy, even though many people deny it, and women essentially invented the modern mystery genre (dang that Agatha Christie!). Writers of color had a tougher time, but when a determined few elbowed their way into Our Kind's gatherings, Our Kind realized they at least needed to publish a few of these books (hence the African American section of U.S. bookstores was formed, ghettoizing the books that should've been on the shelf next to all the other books).

Indie publishing is allowing the creatives to break out of the artificial boxes formed by Our Kind. Women can write strong military SF. African-American writers can write about middle-class lives and middle-class values in the black community instead of being forced to write about the ghetto or voodoo magic (which they might be as unfamiliar with as Our Kind is).

And yet, writers are hearing these arguments that prescribe who should write what, and worse, many writers are believing it.

The gatekeepers are going away, so the loud voices in all the genres are trying to step up as gatekeepers.

It makes me shake my head.

So, for example…

An award seems biased toward a certain kind of writing. So what? Awards are always biased, because they're given by a particular group, and every group—I don't care who runs it—has a particular perspective.

If you don't believe me, watch the Grammys or the Academy Awards every year, and read the analysis about the nominees. I've made a private study of the Oscars since I was a teenager, and what I learned was that the Academy of Motion Picture Arts and Sciences would rather *it* chose the film of the year than let the filmgoers do so.

Not that it matters much. Marvel Comics movies might never win Best Picture, but they always win at the box office.

Recognition is nice, but the best recognition in the world is from the readers themselves. (Which is why I always value Readers' Choice Awards more than some juried award. The readers chose, not five selected gatekeepers taking a vote behind a closed door.)

Writers get so caught up in the "shoulds" and "should nots" that they twist themselves into a pretzel in the worst place possible—their own creativity.

I can remember mentally shouting down that writer-friend who told me I shouldn't write fat fantasy novels. Every time I started a new fantasy novel, I had to silence his voice.

It wasn't until I realized that I wasn't writing to please him or the other gatekeepers that I was finally able to silence his voice entirely.

Because being creative is about flying in the face of accepted wisdom. It's about writing what you want to write, in the way that only you can write it. It's about taking risks and facing down the critics. It's about using forbidden words and writing about topics that, judging by your appearance, you should know nothing about. It's about facing down the bigots who say you've only attracted readers because your last name implies a certain ethnicity.

These people who are screaming at each other on forums and in the media? Those folks? They're not your readers. They're not the people who act as gatekeepers any longer. They have nothing to do with what you write.

What you write is between you and your keyboard.

When that writing is published, it's done. You should move onto another project, and let the published one take care of itself.

You will always be a representative of your time. We all currently hold opinions that future generations will see as quaint (at best) or horribly bigoted (at worst). It might not be possible for you, in the position you're in right now, to know if you even hold such opinions.

If you're one of the screamers, back away from social media. You're only alienating your friends and your readers. If you want to change minds, work on writing better fiction. You can explore all the different points of view in your stories and—oh, yeah—maybe you can learn to write from a point of view not your own.

I love what Ian Rankin has to say about writing from the point of view of his most famous character, John Rebus:

> When I start writing a book, I know I am about to enter a debate with the creature I am bringing to life. My attitudes will not necessarily be his.... _It's fortunate I'll never meet him: I have the feeling we wouldn't get along..._[14]

I don't get along with a lot of my characters. I write from the point of view of mass murderers and psycho criminals, from the point of view of bigoted cops and men who hate women.

I also write from the points of view of African-Americans in the 1970s, Native Americans in 1908 (upcoming), FBI agents from the 1960s, Vietnam veterans and anti-war protestors.

I am none of these people.

I am the writer. And as the writer, I get to choose whose viewpoint I write from. Because my last name is Germanic doesn't mean I always use a German point of view or even a German-American point of view. Just because I'm a woman doesn't mean all my female characters are sympathetic or, indeed, anything like me. Just because I'm white doesn't mean that I agree with all of the white characters in my books.

I write what the story demands. I admit, I'm often using my experiences, my politics, and my opinions as starting points. But they're only *starting* points. I'm often startled where these writing journeys take me. I learn about myself, and in order to write from a point of view not my own, I also have to learn about others.

The best trait *good* writers have is empathy. When writers are trying to shout each other down and demanded that one side write like the other side, they're destroying the empathy—as well as their own creativity.

If you've been watching these fights, and taking in the "shoulds" from these arguers, let me tell you something: The loudest voices here will have to stop arguing at some point or the owners of those loud voices will stop having a career.

The people who didn't like tie-in novels? They're mostly gone. Those who remain have written a few tie-ins themselves.

The fat-fantasy haters? The survivors have written fantasy novels. The rest are gone, including my writer-friend, who hasn't published anything (not even a short story) in decades.

Go ahead, read the history of your favorite genre. You'll often see these fights, and they're often led by people you've never heard of. Do some investigating about those people and you'll learn that they had a great start to a career, and something embittered them, and made them try to control others.

Indie publishing has made writing from different points of view easier, but different points of view have always found their way into print. Take a look at the way the voices of the Harlem Renaissance got published, and remained published. Often we've heard new voices not because they were "discovered" by the gatekeepers, but because these voices self-published or found a small press willing to take a risk with them.

If you as a writer are not willing to take risks, if you're not willing to fly in the face of conventional wisdom, if you're not willing to write what you want—screamers be damned—then why are you writing?

To please others? There are better ways to do that.

Yes, sometimes tackling subjects that others have labeled forbidden is hard. Emotionally and physically hard. But if those subjects interest you, write about them. Embrace the fear, and write.

Writing isn't about doing what everyone else tells you to do.

Writing is about doing what your creative voice *wants* to do.

Learning to tell the difference is sometimes hard. But I can tell you from experience that learning to tell the difference is what good writing is all about.

Don't know how to get those conflicting voices out of your head? Well, sometimes you need a little bit of ego and a whole lot of courage. Here, in this post from 2011, are some examples from the past to guide you along.

CHAPTER TEN

BELIEVE IN YOURSELF

On Tuesday, October 25, 2011, National Public Radio ran a piece titled, "My Accidental Masterpiece: *The Phantom Tollbooth*," by Norton Juster.[15] My sister gave me *The Phantom Tollbooth* when I was a kid. The book is still on my bookshelf, not in the best of condition, with my name badly scrawled on the flyleaf.

I loved the book, and still remember unwrapping it on Christmas morning. (I used to go around and shake packages, like any kid, and then, if the package was a book, I'd set it toward the back of the pile, because I knew books were best.) When I read *The Phantom Tollbooth* and fell in love with it, I had no idea that it was the subject of some controversy.

Juster mentions the controversy with vivid language and with anger at the special insanity that comes from the Folks Who Know Best.

"Not everyone in the publishing world of the 1960s embraced *The Phantom Tollbooth*," Juster writes. "Many said it was not a children's book, the vocabulary was much too difficult, and the ideas were beyond kids. To top it off, they claimed fantasy was bad for children because it distorts them.

"The prevailing wisdom of the time was that learning should be more accessible and less discouraging. The aim was that no child would ever have to confront anything that he or she didn't already know."

The NPR piece is thirteen paragraphs long, and would take about a minute to read out loud (or so my former radio work tells me). The piece celebrates the fiftieth anniversary of a book that has become a classic.

Juster uses two of those paragraphs to remember the negative reception the book received, and another to refute that reception directly.

He writes, "But my feeling is that there is no such thing as a difficult word. There are only words you don't know yet—the kind of liberating words that Milo [the book's main character] encounters on his adventure."

In that paragraph, you can hear both the bafflement at the critiques the book initially received and the determination that made Juster keep the book exactly the way he wanted it to be. Juster believed in his own vision—still believes in that vision—and he didn't compromise it.

The fact that the book became a classic must be icing on that proverbial cake for him.

He probably considered it a miracle that the book got published at all.

The publishing world of the late 1950s and early 1960s was different than the one we find ourselves in today. It was less corporate. Editors had more power. There were more traditional publishing houses who competed with each other But that didn't make things any easier for writers.

In fact, things were much tougher for writers then than they are in 2011. In the 1950s, if all the publishing doors closed on a project, then that project was effectively dead. Of course, back then you had hundreds of doors to try before you declared that book dead.

The world of children's literature was particularly tough at the time because of these strange prejudices that filled the field, prejudices that had existed since children's literature became its own branch of publishing in the 1920s. The baby boom provided opportunity: So many children wanted books that the field was growing, and new voices got heard.

Theodor Geisel, whom you all know as Dr. Seuss, stunned the publishing world by writing an original and somewhat controversial book for a strict formula book line. He had the task of writing a children's book, using only 225 approved words. None of those words could be more than two syllables.

He ended up using most of the approved words, threw in a few of his own, and added just one word of three syllables. Even though the finished book was less than 2,000 words long, it took him eight months to finish it because he found it so hard to write with such stringent limitations.

He turned in *The Cat in the Hat* to his editors at Houghton Mifflin and Random House (who worked on the project jointly for contractual reasons), and then had to suffer through some ridiculous criticism. The book, you see, promoted terrible behavior. That amoral cat taught the children how to act badly while their parents were away.

I have no idea how many fights Geisel had to conduct to keep his book as he wanted it, but I do know that the arguments about the "lessons" that *The Cat in the Hat* teaches continues to this day. I heard them resurrected when *The Cat in the Hat* movie came out a few years ago.

Once again, The Guardians of Quality and Those Who Know Better deemed *The Cat in the Hat* a book (and movie) that might unduly harm children. Only now, fifty-plus years after the book's initial publication, *The Cat in the Hat* is such a beloved classic that those of us who read the book as children and have read the book to children laugh at such silly criticism.

Another writer toiling in the children's literature departments of publishing houses in the 1950s was the science fiction author Robert A. Heinlein. Heinlein, who is now considered one of the giants of the science fiction field, wrote what were then called juveniles (but which would now be called Middle Grade) novels with an eye toward Christmas publication. He published twelve juveniles between 1947 and 1958, books that revolutionized not just the juvenile market, but the science fiction field. Every major SF writer and editor between the ages of forty and sixty working today read the juveniles, and cites their influence (either positive or negative).

At a Wiscon science fiction convention many years ago, I was the Editor Guest of Honor when Lois McMaster Bujold was the Writer Guest of Honor. Lois spent one evening in the con suite (a gathering place for convention goers) reading aloud from the books that Scribner's had published before the company hired Heinlein to write the books. The previous books were sad and pretentious and (quite frankly) dull, but filled with things that a child "already knew" even though the books were (supposedly) about families going into space. These books made the TV show *Lost in Space*, which aired nearly two decades later, seem like great innovative intellectual fodder.

We laughed our way through that evening, and more than once, someone in the room expressed gratitude that Heinlein had been hired to replace that abysmal writer. At the time, I did not know that Heinlein had parted from Scribner's and the juveniles over a book.

After writing twelve of these books, Heinlein turned in his annual manuscript, and then got told that Scribner's could not accept the new novel. I haven't bothered to see if he was invited to write a new book or if his contract with Scribner's was effectively canceled. Either way, the end result was the same. The famous line of Heinlein juveniles ended when Scribner's bounced that novel.

The novel was Heinlein's Hugo-Award-winning classic, *Starship Troopers*. The book remains controversial to this day. It was particularly out of step with children's literature at the time: It was about young people going to war. The controversy remains: The 1997 movie of the same name caused a lot of debate—not because of its effect on children, but because of its message.

The science fiction field as we know it would not exist without Heinlein's juveniles or Heinlein himself. *Starship Troopers* remains one of the classics in the field. Heinlein did not try to revise the book to editorial guidelines, nor did he dumb it down in order to sell it.

The Easy Reader aspect of the children's book field would not be the same without *The Cat in the Hat*. It remains an enjoyable, if uneasy, book, designed for children to read on their own. Without *The Cat in the Hat*, we would have no *Where the Wild Things Are*, no modern children's literature at all.

As I once (angrily) told an agent who refused to market an unusual book of mine, the books that make a difference aren't the books that imitate other books. The books that make a difference, the books that have long-lasting impact—hell, the books that often hit the top of bestseller lists for the first time for their authors—aren't clones of some other book. From *Presumed Innocent* to *The Exorcist*, *Starship Troopers* to *The Cat in the Hat*, the books that changed how we think about genre and literature and *reading* are originals—things we as readers have never encountered before.

The American publishing culture has lost sight of this truism if, indeed, it ever really knew it. It's easier to sell a book that reminds you of another book. You can cross-compare. This is how the very idea of segregating bookstores into genre sections came about: Genre, however imperfect, became a way to define books without reading them.

It is no coincidence that the rise in genre marketing matched the rise in the quantity of books published. There came a point when no one could read every book published in a single year—a good thing, in my opinion.

Over the years, we have drilled down this notion of genre into something so fine that we have subgenres, and sub-subgenres, and breakout genres. (Thriller, for example, used to be a sub-genre of mystery. Now thriller is a breakout genre—meaning it broke out of its label—and has become a much bigger-selling genre than mystery.) It is to the point that if you want to sell a novel into traditional publishing, you must not only know the genre the book belongs to, but its subgenre as well. In fact, in your pitch letter, you must tell the editor what other books your novel is similar to and if you are wrong, then that's an easy rejection.

All of that is, in my opinion, the cost of working with a large publishing company. You the writer are making a deal with that company: You will provide a marketable novel in exchange for the distribution and marketing. You will invest your time (and therefore your dollars, since time is money) on creating a salable product and the publishing company will invest its resources into getting that book to market.

It can cost large publishers as much as $250,000 per title to get their books to market. That includes overhead, shipping, warehousing, production, editing services, advertising, the advance, and more. Inside that overhead is not just the rent for the office space, but the salaries of the editor, sales force, managing editor, and others who worked on that book. Those salaries are divided down into a formula that works out to some kind of hourly figure which then becomes a cost on the balance sheet for one novel.

Publishers reject books all the time that the sales force believes cannot earn back that $250,000 cost of production. That's smart business: It makes no sense to take on 500-page rhymed ode to a snail that will sell to the author's family (and snail lovers everywhere) when a 300-page fast-moving thriller in the style of James Patterson will probably sell better.

The lesson to writers is pretty simple: If you write a 500-page rhymed ode to a snail, you should accept that no one in traditional publishing will be interested in your work.

However, you can self-publish the work now, and prove (me and) those folks in traditional publishing's sales force wrong, by showing that there is indeed a large snail- and poetry-loving book-buying population out there. We as writers have that option now.

Which brings me to my surprise after my post titled "R*E*S*P*E*C*T."[16] For those of you who missed it, I got quite angry last week at some disrespectful treatment on the part of two editors. One editor's treatment was probably simple thoughtlessness; the other editor's treatment led to near-legal battles and a lot of negotiation, resulting in a contract cancellation.

I wrote about how common the lack of respect happens to be for writers who work in traditional publishing. I received great e-mails, letters, and comments from a lot of you about my work in particular and about the treatment in general. Thank you for all the encouragement and support, although I must say that I was writing to vent, not to elicit compliments.

I also saw a lot of blog posts from other long-term professional writers linking to my post, and detailing similar experiences. One writer whom I admire greatly and who has been in the field longer than I have expressed surprise that I (with all of my multi-genre and publishing experience) was subjected to the same mistreatment that "the rest of us have suffered over the years."

The comment made me sad and made me have a similar re-action to his with me. How did anyone manage to mistreat that particular writer given the awards, publishing experience, and high quality of his work? It's an outrageous thing and something writers do not and should not ever have to put up with.

Mingled with my surprise at the sheer number of recognizable names who wrote me to tell me of similar experiences was the most common response from published and unpublished writers alike.

They seemed surprised that I stood up for myself.

And that shocks me deeply, given what I have just outlined above.

Did Norton Juster, Theodor Geisel, and Robert Heinlein be-come huge successes because they wrote great work? Or because they refused to back down when pushed?

I contend that it was both.

Too many writers revise continually in order to sell their books. Beginning writers revise a novel a dozen times because their writers' workshop (which usually does not include a single publishing professional) has told them to. Midlist writers revise to their agent's suggestion because the agent believes the novel is "unsalable" as is—impossible to market because the novel is too different from anything else. Bestsellers listen to their publisher's desire to have a book just like the last book, eventually making the bestseller's work predictable and dull.

Most writers of all levels do not stand up for their work be-cause they're afraid they'll never sell another word. They're afraid to take a risk which—in my mind—begs the question: If you're unwilling to take a risk, why become a writer in the first place?

Writing is all about risk. The first risk is comes in putting the first word on paper, in believing that you are good enough to at-tract readers. The second risk is working in the arts in America, which has always been a dicey proposition. The third risk is be-lieving that your vision matters.

The moment you lose your integrity, you lose your vision. If you lose your vision, you lose what makes you unique as a writer.

Should you learn craft? Of course. You need to learn how to tell the best story possible. You need to learn the tools of storytelling. You should not focus on the words, but on the unique way that you see the world. Everything in your writing should be in service of the story you are trying to tell, be that story a thriller in the traditional of James Patterson or a 500-page rhymed ode to a snail.

You must constantly work to improve your craft. You must strive to get better, and never assume that you know everything there is to know about writing or storytelling. You must always write to the best of your ability.

When you are done telling your story, when it is the best it can be, that's when you worry about marketing. You do not write to market. You write *and then* find a market that might publish your work. Should you market to a traditional publisher? Should you self-publish? Should you go with a small regional press?

Those questions have no easy answer. It doesn't matter how many times you folks email me asking me to make the decision for you. I can't. It's a personal decision these days, a decision made possible by the ease with which writers now can distribute their own work. You can self-publish, prove that there is a market, and traditional publishers will come calling. It will then become your choice as to whether or not you sign with them.

(I do suggest that you learn business, money management, and copyright before you make any decisions. Because choosing between traditional publishing and indie publishing is, at heart, a business decision.)

So, am I telling you to stand up for yourself because you now have the option of self publishing?

Hell, no. I would have told you this twenty years ago. In fact, I have always told writers this.

Note my examples above. They all took place around the time I was born. Robert A. Heinlein walked away from a lucrative career writing juveniles because he believed in *Starship Troopers*. Who knows how many rejections Norton Juster suffered? I do know that Theodor Geisel expected *The Cat in the Hat* to get rejected (and it nearly was), but that didn't stop him from writing the book he wanted and subverting the formula the publishing company had given him.

What's shocking, folks, is not that I stand up for myself. What's shocking is that most of you didn't even realize standing up for yourself was an option.

Write the best work you possibly can. Then *believe* in that work and in yourself. It's your vision, not the publishing company's or the agent's or the sales force's. Believe me, if the publishing company or the agent or the sales force could write a novel that sold millions of copies, they would. They don't know how to do it. In fact, they know so little about it that they discourage the very thing that creates classics: originality.

Originality is all that you have. As one of my college creative writing professors said on the first day of class, "There are seven plots. Shakespeare wrote them better than anyone. If that scares you, leave now."

If you are unwilling to stand up for yourself, you are in the wrong profession. Believe in yourself. Because at various points in your writing career, the only person you will have on your side is you.

If Norton Juster hadn't believed in himself, I would not have a battered and beloved copy of *The Phantom Tollbooth* on my shelf. If Robert A. Heinlein had not believed in himself, most of science fiction would not exist.

Could those men see the impact they would have on publishing? Of course not. They just knew they had a good book, and

they believed in it—enough that they walked away when someone wanted to cut the heart out of the book itself.

Apparently many writers today are unwilling to make that choice.

And that's a shame, because it's so much easier to stand up for
yourself now. We have so many options.

If you only open your eyes and look.

I tell you to believe in yourself. I tell you to stand up for yourself. Easy for me to say, right? And besides, most of you know how to deal with external problems. You tell people they've crossed a line.

But what happens when those people invade your mind? When their opinions just won't leave? What happens when you sit down to write and the doubts these people planted in your brain surface?

I have a simple and effective trick for that, one I explained in this post from 2013.

CHAPTER ELEVEN

OUT! ALL OF YOU!

As those of you who read this blog regularly know, I have a magpie brain. I find shiny things here and there, and then I put them together—not to create a nest (I have one, thanks)—but to help me form a realization or to figure out the solution to a problem or to reinforce things I already know.

I have been reading Peter Guralnick's *Lost Highway*, a collection of his 1970s essays on music—from blues to rockabilly to country. *Lost Highway* collects articles he wrote about musicians from Rufus Thomas to Hank Snow. Art is art is art, and musicians are artists, just like writers, struggling with the business and trying to hang onto their creativity in the face of difficult economic forces.

I picked up the book because I love Guralnick's writing. He has a way of making music and musicians come alive. His two-volume biography of Elvis Presley is one of the best biographies I've ever read, and his book on Sam Cooke is equally impressive.

These essays, written earlier in his career, show the same talents that informed his bestselling biographies.

The essays also form a snapshot in time. Written as the music industry was completing its change from regional performers to national hit makers, the essays occasionally lapse into an argument I haven't heard in more than thirty years.

Every artist in this book has an audience, Guralnick wrote in 1979, *every artist in this book has a* mass *audience— whether of five thousand, fifty thousand, or even half a million—but that is not enough. In order for a record to be successful, it has to sell millions. In order for a performer to be successful, he has to appear on the* Johnny Carson Show. *In order to appear on network television, it is necessary to appeal to the lowest common denominator; all regional identification must be smoothed over.... If Elvis came along today, you have the feeling, he would not get the airplay, simply because he was, well—too strange, too out of the ordinary.*[17]

And there is some truth to that. Music that appeals to millions of people sounds different than music that appeals to an educated or traditionalist few. But, as Guralnick points out over and over again, it's the originals, the artists who have a flat sound or make a banjo sound like a harp, who inspire other artists. He begins the entire book with a short essay on Jimmie Rodgers, because he felt—even then!—that his readers had no idea who Rodgers was.

I hadn't heard of Rodgers until I heard the Alannah Myles hit, "Black Velvet," about Elvis Presley. The first verse mentions baby Elvis on his mother's shoulder as she plays Jimmie Rodgers on the Victrola. If you look up the lyrics, you'll see that most transcriptions misspell both of Rodgers' names. He's not well known any longer, but he was in his time. He died in 1933, after influencing musicians as diverse as Elvis, Howlin' Wolf, and Gene Autry.

What goes around comes around, however. Now, the music industry discusses how impossible it is to appeal to that "lowest common denominator," that the age of million-selling albums is over. Many artists, who came of age in their industry after 1980, lament the loss. Other, younger artists see the potential of the new system.

As Maroon 5 lead singer Adam Levine said in *Vanity Fair*:

> *The diversity in people's tastes now is so much cooler. Everyone is saying MP3s and the Internet have ruined the music business—and it's sad there are no record stores—but music is just so present now in the culture. More than it's ever been. That's a result of the [technological] advancements we've made. I'm such a huge fan of where music is right now.*[18]

I am too, just like I'm a fan of the diversity that's springing up in the publishing business. *RT Book Reviews* had a recent article[19] on a new publishing category that they call New Adult—something between adult fiction and young adult fiction, dealing with college-aged protagonists. Apparently, traditional publishing felt books with college-aged protagonists did not sell, until indie-published writers proved that myth wrong.

The audience is there. It's just impossible for the suits and sales forces to recognize something new, or to see the value in something older, something that isn't the flavor of the month.

The older artists in Guralnick's book talk about the things we discuss on my blog—surviving in changing times. Their world was falling away. At the time of the book's first publication in 1979, Ernest Tubb had been dropped by his record label after forty years because he wouldn't change with the times. But he still had his fan base, and he was still making music. He wasn't happy, but he was rolling with the punches.

That's what it takes to have a long-time career. But it takes more than an ability to pick yourself up after each knockout punch. You also need to believe in yourself with a fierce passion. You need to know that your vision is the correct vision *for you*, and then you need to defend it.

I started the Guralnick book the same day Sally Field was interviewed on *Nightline*. She told a story she has told a hundred times before. I'd read it, but I'd never seen her tell the story. I've put the link in the endnotes.[20] Watch her face, starting at the 2:45 minute mark. You'll see a fierce woman, who defended herself at great cost.

Defended herself against what? you might ask.

Against her agents, her business manager, and her then-husband. In 1972, Field wanted to go from television—oh, let's be honest here; from being typecast as the beloved airhead Gidget to a career in the movies. Her agents told her she wasn't pretty enough or good enough.

Field's response? "You're fired."

You're fired.

She didn't bow her cute little head and listen to their advice. She didn't let them bully her. She left her agents, her manager, and her husband (who agreed with them). She ends the anecdote with this:

[That time] was like 'Out! All of you!'

Four very important words.

Out! All of you!

All of you who don't believe, who offer bad advice under the cloak of good advice. Who recommend that something innovative get tossed because it is unusual. Better to blend in, better to try to be like everyone else. All of you who are afraid of risks. You—out!

Field has had a fascinating career, filled with ups and downs, but she's not the only long-time actor who took risks.

My third little example from my weekend of examples is from the *Los Angeles Times*.[21] In an interview with Bruce Willis strategically timed to go with his latest movie, the *Times* shares this little nugget of wisdom:

> *Industry observers think that [Willis's] longevity over the last three decades as a die-hard working man's actor can largely be attributed to one thing: diversity of roles and types of movies.*

How did Willis end up with those diverse roles in an unpredictable grouping of films? He listened to advice, but made decisions for himself. After he had become a successful action hero, he says, he wanted to play supporting roles too. His agent told him "Don't do it. You'll ruin your career."

Instead, Willis guaranteed that he has a career at fifty-eight. Yes, he still does action, but not exclusively. His two old friends Sylvester Stallone and Arnold Schwarzenegger had action films die at the box office this year, while the fifth *Die Hard* movie, *A Good Day To Die Hard*, hit number one on its opening weekend. Even if the movie hadn't hit number one, it wouldn't have mattered to Willis's career. He had six films come out in 2012 alone.

He also brought very little vanity to his approach to the roles. When he took a small part in one of my favorite movies, *Nobody's Fool* (based on an equally wonderful Richard Russo novel), he did so in order to work with Paul Newman.

His agent, clearly distressed, told Willis that they didn't have a billing for him in the credits. Lacking a billing doesn't mean that they couldn't be bothered to put his name on the film. What it means is that they couldn't *pay* him to put his name in the proper place for a movie star on the credits. Each slot, especially above the title (which was where the Willis name should have gone) brings with it extra money—sometimes a lot of extra money.

Willis's response to the agent? *"I said, 'I don't need a billing.' He said, 'You're out of your mind.' Later, [Paul] Newman called me and said, 'That's the [gutsiest] thing I've heard anyone say for a long time.'"*

And that gutsy thing is why these days the *LA Times* is comparing Bruce Willis to Academy-Award-winner Michael Caine, not to Sylvester Stallone. Caine, who has acted (bit parts to starring roles) in more than one hundred films so far.

Sally Field displayed the same gutsiness. Imagine how hard it was for twenty-something Field, mother of two and the family breadwinner, to tell her agents, manager, and husband to take a flying—well, not nun. That gutsiness brought her Oscars and Emmys as well as an Oscar nomination for a role this year that she had to fight to get. She had to prove to Steven Spielberg that she was right to play Mary Todd Lincoln. If she hadn't fought, he wouldn't have cast her.

What these biographies and feel-good stories don't tell you is the difficult times between the "Out! All of You!" and the next success. Think about this: Field fired her entire support crew in 1972 and worked on rebuilding. It couldn't have been easy. I'm sure that she had almost daily doubts about the choices she had made. And those doubts probably lasted for the four years between the firings and her next success. That success was in 1976, as the title character in the TV movie *Sybil*. But her true vindication didn't occur until she won an Oscar for her role as the title character of the movie, *Norma Rae*.

I'm sure the fired agents, manager, and husband were surprised.

Was that vindication enough? Probably not. Because if you choose to remain active in the arts—to have a lifelong career—

you can't rest on your laurels. If you do, you'll become that actress—you know, the one who won the Oscar for playing that woman union organizer? You know. Her.

To avoid the whatever-happened-to fate, you have to prove yourself—or reinvent yourself—over and over again.

Sometimes you do it, not because you fired your support team or because you decided to work with Paul Newman (sigh), but because the industry has changed around you.

Guralnick talks about the changes in music in-depth in his profile of Ernest Tubb. Tubb, without his original label, reinvented himself a second time (the first was in the 1950s). As an article on legacy.com[22] says quite succinctly:

> But as he'd always done, Tubb weathered audience vicissitudes, relying on a loyal fan base he'd built over 30 years. Constantly on the road, he reportedly logged 3 million miles on his tour bus from 1970-1979.

He did what he had to in order to maintain his career and the music he loved. I would wager some suit told him to learn what was then called "countrypolitan" music—the so-called "sophisticated" music that had risen to the top of the country charts in those days—and I'll wager that was one of the many reasons Tubb and his label parted ways.

An artist must remain true to himself, if he plans to remain an artist.

It's the only way to survive.

I have to remind myself of it repeatedly. Oscar season helps, because it's usually filled with stories like Sally Field's—an acclaimed, award-winning actress, nearly denied a role that she would triumph in because someone didn't see her that way. Or Willis, choosing to play a rather despicable character for little money and no credit, just to stand side by side with (and presumably learn from) Paul Newman.

I'm thinking about the ebbs and flows of careers a lot lately because the changes in publishing are allowing me to revive and/or finish old series. I know why I had to quit writing most of them. Early on, I took the loss of each series personally, figuring I had made a mistake. Eventually, I realized I was becoming one of the many casualties of an earlier change in publishing—the one Guralnick decried that happened in music in the 1970s.

Parts of my work had become widgets that didn't have a high enough sales volume to reach the mass audience the corporations needed to keep up their hefty bottom lines. Other things I wrote did just fine; they made that sales volume.

But those things forced me into a series of ever smaller boxes, the idea that I *should* write only certain things, even though I wanted—and was capable of—writing several other kinds of things. To make matters worse, many of those boxes formed because other opportunities died because of someone else's incompetence, or simple dumb luck. It wasn't because I was best at the things I ended up doing; it was because those were the things that had had better breaks.

It all seemed random, and that made it even more frustrating.

And then there was the changing role of advisors. Instead of making wry commentary like Bruce Willis's agents, mine were treating me like Sally Field's treated her. One agent flat-out told me I wasn't talented enough to write in genres other than science fiction. Another wrote a cover letter on one of my manuscripts that he had mailed to an editor, apologizing for the submission because it was clear to both of them I couldn't write, but admitting that I had forced him into mailing the book anyway.

I wasn't as bold as Sally Field in the case of the first agent: I didn't fire her right away, although I eventually did. In the case of the second: I didn't find out what he had done until I had fired him for other reasons and then I got copies of all the correspondence.

Somewhere along the way, the advisors felt they should control my career rather than allowing me to control it. All of this was before 2007, and since then things have only gotten worse.

Only instead of saying "Out! All of you!" to advisors like that, most writers embrace the criticism or the snide comments, and try to shove themselves into the tiny boxes, not realizing that they're destroying the one thing that makes them unique.

Dean and I have moved back into what we call our teaching season again. We teach to pay forward, since we can't repay our own marvelous instructors for the boost they gave us—at least not in any meaningful way. All we can do is offer the same kind of assistance to a new generation of writers.

What disturbs me every teaching season is the way that writers wait for someone to tell them what box they fit in or what box they should go to. Every year, writers tell at least one of us that we need to give them better instructions. If we give better instructions, the writers insist, then they can write what we want them to write, so that we'll be happy with them.

These writers entirely miss the point. The point isn't for *us* to be happy, but for those writers to find their own voice. Sometimes they'll fail an assignment and have to do it all over again from scratch. Oh, well. All that means is that they have to invest more time into their craft.

But for a certain type of writer, it means that they have screwed up completely, that they'll never succeed, that they didn't receive the help they needed to mold themselves into something someone else wanted.

We can't help those writers. We try not to teach them, because we teach writers to stand on their own, defend their own vision, and become who *they* want to be, not who they're told to be. It's a tougher road to walk, because it means that there's no one to blame when things go wrong.

Yeah, I get it. Up above, I said that series of mine failed, sometimes because of someone else's incompetence. When I'm talking about that, I'm only discussing the business side of the equation—sending me on a book tour, but failing to provide books or to fulfill orders from bookstores. Refusing to do a second printing on a book that was nominated for half a dozen awards because "it wasn't time" for a second printing yet (whatever that meant) even though there were orders for the book.

When a book sold poorly because of something I could control—the wrong pacing for a certain genre, being ten years ahead of a trend (which is common for me), tackling a difficult subject that no one wants to read about except maybe me, I take responsibility for that. And I should.

But I also know that those failed projects have helped me grow into a stronger writer. If I don't reach for the impossible, if I don't stretch and write what frightens me each and every day, I'm failing as a writer.

Failing as an artist, really. Because all long-time successful artists talk about the same thing. If they aren't frightened at the beginning of a project, if they're not worried lacking the ability to do a scene or a story justice, then they're not stretching themselves. And artists who don't stretch eventually become artists who stop improving.

The most important thing an artist can do when she's working is to clear out all of the naysaying voices. Sure, someone told you that you can't write from the point of view on an unlikeable person. Try it anyway. Sure, someone told you that books about college students don't sell. Write whatever you want to write.

An agent told a friend of mine that teens don't buy books longer than 200 pages. When my friend pointed out the last few

Harry Potter books, all weighing in at 600-plus pages, the agent said, "Well, that's Harry Potter." As if J.K. Rowling hadn't been a beginner once. As if teens weren't buying those books.

The world's worst editor told me one afternoon that I couldn't mix science fiction, romance, and mystery. I had to write a romance with "trappings" of the others, but not the plots. I said, "What about J.D. Robb? Her books sell." "Well," the world's worst editor responded, "That's Nora Roberts. Of course, she sells." And so I started listing all the other writers whose work fell into all three categories. "You're not them," the world's worst editor snapped.

Nope, I wasn't. And maybe my crossover fiction didn't work because the manuscripts were flawed. But the world's worst editor didn't even want to try marketing that work because it was "different."

I found another editor. I write crossover fiction all the time.

But if I'd let that voice into my head, into my work space, I would have stopped writing crossover fiction, which is 90% of what I write. Sometimes you have to fire the person who gives you bad advice or leave them or just walk away from the publishing house.

Most of the time, however, you need to clear those voices out of your head.

The best way to do it is exactly what Sally Field said: *Out! All of you!*

Watch that little segment. See her tone, her half smile, feel the passion in those words spoken in reminiscence of an event forty years in her past. She doesn't regret what she did, and she's still angry about what they said.

As she should be.

Fight for yourself with that same kind of tenacity.

It's the only way you'll have a long career. It's the only way you'll survive.

Does it matter how you define yourself? I don't think so. Once again, a definition puts you in a box. You're better off figuring out what kind of writer you want to be. And I hope this last chapter, originally published in 2012, will give you a starting point toward figuring that out.

CHAPTER TWELVE

THE WRITER YOU WANT TO BE

This past week, Dean tilted at a windmill and decided to define terms in this new world of publishing.[23] He defined indie publishers as writers who have started a press to publish their work and maybe the work of others. (In other words, if you saw the book on Amazon, you'd see: *The Story* by Writer A. Published by Some Press.)

Specialty presses, according to Dean, publish high-quality, often limited-edition books, and have been around forever. He defined small presses as "a term used in the larger world of publishing to define a publisher, either an indie or a specialty publisher, who has gross sales under a certain figure. That figure tends to be around 50 million dollars. Or less than ten titles per year."

Then he defines the publishing industry that we used to know—those big multinational corporations—as traditional publishing. I like those terms as well, and agree with what he said in the piece.

Why do I say he is tilting at windmills? Because writers need something to argue about and so do publishers. Right now, independent presses that have been around for years are angry at the "co-opting" of the term "indie" by "self-published" writers who "have no idea what they're doing."

Actually, the real problem that those long-term independent presses have is that they're no longer special. Back when it was hard to get a book published outside of the traditional publishing venues, the independent press provided an essential service. It rescued all kinds of low-selling books from obscurity, making certain that they at least got the critical recognition that they deserved.

Now that publishing has become easier (note that I did not say "easy." It's not easy publishing anything, your own work or someone else's), the old independent presses have lost a lot of cachet. Some have fantastic reputations and to be published by them is a complete honor in and of itself. As long as those presses continue to have a consistent, strong editorial vision, they'll remain important.

But they'll have to share the name "indie" with a whole bunch of up-and-coming presses, some run by writers, others run by brand-new publishers who see a new way of publishing books that they believe should be in the marketplace.

In an area where there's been no competition, the arrival of competitors is threatening. But it's something that the older independent presses will have to get used to. (Some of them also need to change their business model; they'll need to publish e-books, use POD on their trade titles, and stop warehousing the lower-end books. The indies will save money that way and guarantee their own survival.)

Dean has gotten some pushback on this piece, but not so much on his blog. People don't argue with him in public, preferring to yell behind his back. (They do that to me too. I think that silly; if you have an argument, defend it.)

He and I were talking about some of that pushback the other night, and he said to me that he was no longer sure where he fit in his own categories. Together, we co-founded WMG Publishing, which has already grown to three employees (not us), plus a ton of support staff. We've got several other businesses, some related to WMG, some not.

WMG is a corporation; it is not us. So we have publishing contracts with WMG, as will other writers as the years go on. Our anthology series, *Fiction River*, will contract with dozens of writers in the next year or so, but the contract will come from WMG, which owns *Fiction River*. And so on.

Dean said to me, with a bit of surprise, "I think I'm no longer a self-published writer." So I pointed at his blog, and said, "You self-publish every single week."

He looked a bit sheepish. "Oh, yeah," he said. "That's right."

And the conversation between us ended. But I didn't stop thinking about it. I took a good hard look at my own writing career and tried to figure out who I was and how I fit into all of those categories.

Here's what's going on as best as I can figure:

I publish novels through more than one traditional publishing company in the United States alone. If you add my novel publications overseas, I'm with dozens of traditional publishing companies with a variety of works.

I publish short stories through even more traditional publishing venues, from fiction magazines (online and in print) to anthologies all over the world.

I publish nonfiction through traditional publishing companies as well as online in several markets—more than I realized until I finally had to admit to myself that yes, I am a nonfiction writer too. Or rather, still. I never did quit writing nonfiction, even though it stopped making my full-time living in the 1980s.

I publish novels through the independent press. If we look at Dean's definition of small press, then WMG has been one for years. Its gross isn't as high as that 50 million—yet—but that'll come. There's a lot of money to be made in publishing, which is why traditional publishers stay in business and why scammers have flocked to it in recent years.

I publish short stories through the independent press as well. I have had collections recently in specialty press venues (not WMG) and online with specialty presses.

I have returned to editing through a specialty press (and honestly, I did some freelance editing without getting credit for it for years. I would rescue editing projects).

And then I self-publish. I've done this blog every week since April 2009. I occasionally put up a short story here. I'm flirting with podcasting, although at the moment that's under WMG's auspices, but who knows what tomorrow might bring? And I have a few projects I don't discuss that I publish myself in venues I don't talk about.

In other words, as a writer, I don't just straddle two areas of publishing—traditional and indie—I straddle three. I'm a traditionally published writer who also publishes with indie presses and who manages to find time to self-publish a few things as well.

And you know what? I've always done that. I write what I write and publish it in the place where I hope/think it will thrive the best. I'm still stunned that I'm better off doing the business books as a blog first. I have sold more copies of the actual books (paper and e-book) than I ever would have sold through a traditional nonfiction press, especially with commercial press limitations on how long the book would be on the shelf.

Still, Dean's attempt at a definition of the various kinds of publishing brings to mind something else: how writers seem to crave being labeled. It used to be that we labeled ourselves as genre writers or nongenre writers, fiction writers or nonfiction writers. Only a few of us tried to cross those lines.

Now we have to add a description of how we're published—and we fight over what that means.

Just today, a friend wrote to me about the fact that some writers whom she points to this blog won't listen to anything that I have to say because everything I do "applies only to genre writers." I could find a lot to argue about with that statement. For one thing, I'll wager I have more mainstream publications than the people making that snobby judgment and I'll wager I've been nominated for more literary (non-genre) awards than they have as well.

But that aside, the definitions—hastily made and held firmly—allow people to dismiss anything that doesn't fit into their worldview.

It limits them more than it limits those of us who don't need the definitions.

As I wrote this piece, I read an essay called "The Writing Life: Editors & Publisher" by John McPhee in *The New Yorker*.[24] He has a lovely digression about the development of writers. He mentions that the *New Yorker*'s famous editor, William Shawn, "once remarked that he thought young writers were 'taking longer to find out what kinds of writers they are…'"

The sentence made McPhee stop and ruminate, and it did the same for me. Here's a bit of what McPhee wrote:

The writing impulse seeks its own level and isn't always given a chance to find it. You can't make up your mind in a Comp Lit class that you're going to be a Russian novelist. Or even an American novelist. Or a poet. Young writers find out what kinds of writers they are by experiment.

He's so right. And experiment takes a variety of forms. He talks a bit about the writing forms:

It is so easy to misjudge yourself and get stuck in the wrong genre. You avoid that, early on, by writing in every genre. If you are telling yourself you're a poet, write poems. Write a lot of poems. If fewer than one work out, throw them all away; you're not a poet. Maybe you're a novelist. You won't know until you have written several novels.

One of the best things Dean and I do as teachers is something we stumbled on accidentally. I got tired of using movies or television as examples of storytelling. I decided all of my students would work off the same fictional templates. So I would assign stories (or novels) in a variety of genres for every class that I taught. Early on, one of the students realized that she was writing in the wrong genre; that she liked novels published in a genre she never read. She switched to that genre and now has a long (and successful) career there.

I had thought she was an aberration, but time proved me wrong. Many writers have no idea what genre they belong in because they read only one genre. They get stuck in that genre. Many writers have no idea what their strengths are. We all know our weaknesses because critique focuses on problems, but most of us have no idea what we do well.

Now apply this same theory to Dean's list above. In the not-so-distant past, we all had only one road to publishing success. We had to go through traditional publishers. Some writers, like me, spread out our opportunities by writing nonfiction articles as well as fiction in the short story and novel form, but we still went the traditional route to publication.

Then the easy access to e-books and print-on-demand publishing happened, and our opportunities are endless. We can have a hybrid career like mine above or we can focus just on traditional or we can be 100% self-published. We can start our own publishing businesses or we can write for someone else's business.

It's really up to us.

The problem comes, in the words of William Shawn, in "finding out what kind of writer" we are. It takes a long time to figure out what interests us in subject matter; it might take longer to figure out where we're the most comfortable publishing that subject matter.

So many writers default to traditional because that's what they know. They're like my former student, struggling in a system that they're familiar with, but one which might not be a good fit for them. Yet they're unwilling to try anything new.

And by being unwilling to try something new, they're limiting not just their choices, but what kind of writer they can be. Maybe they write quirky offbeat stuff that's doomed to small print runs in traditional houses, but would do extremely well in a self-publishing system. After all, those quirky books would stay in print, sell all over the world, and build an audience slowly, which is what quirky usually does.

Or maybe they have such a commercial book that they could be the next John Grisham if it finds the right home. They might not have the opportunity to have a huge impact on the culture with everyone talking about the same book at the same time if they don't try a traditional publishing route.

What writers have to remember in business is that they can just say no. So you think you're the next John Grisham. You take your book to a traditional house and they only offer you a midlist contract, not the bestselling deal you want. Say, "No thank you," and walk away. Try a few other traditional houses and if they don't fulfill your bestseller dream, *then* publish the book yourself. Or create an independent press to publish it for you, and build your own name.

Experiment, as McPhee urges. Or don't take his word for it. This advice has been something writers have told each other for at least four hundred years. In his essay, McPhee quotes Shakespeare contemporary, the poet and playwright Ben Jonson, who wrote, "Though a man be more prone and able for one kind of writing than another, he must exercise all." McPhee adds, "Gender aside, I take that to be a message to all young writers."

I think it's a message for all writers. Exercise all of your options. Try new things. Don't worry about how to define yourself. Defining yourself limits you.

Worry about whether or not you've given a different genre enough of a try or whether you've put the right amount of effort into figuring out how to properly publish that story you wrote.

If you look at what you're doing bit by bit, piece by piece, you'll probably end up with the same kind of hybrid that I have. A bit of traditional here, some indie there, a little self-publishing in the middle. You might end up with a preference—I know that Dean's enjoying the hell out of his indie-publishing projects right now—and that preference might remain the same for the rest of your career.

Or it might not. One other thing I experienced in the e-mail today is a short discussion of the future with two of WMG's employees. We tabled a discussion of a new project until the spring because we simply do not have the time to do it.

By then, I joked, things might have changed dramatically. No joke, one of the employees said. Think how different things were *last* spring. She's exactly right. I would never have been expecting to be sitting here eighteen months ago. If you had asked me, I would have guessed that it would have taken five years to get to this position.

Things are changing very fast. Too fast for me to try everything, but I'm keeping an eye out. I believe what John McPhee,

Ben Jonson, and William Shawn were discussing; I think it takes a long time for a writer to figure out what kind of writer she is.

I think it might take a lifetime.

And I hope to remain passionately undefined through it all.

FINAL WORD

As you can tell from the previous twelve chapters, the best way to defeat whatever comes at you when it comes time to write is to remember who you are and how much you love writing.

Even though I wrote these chapters as blog posts over a period of four years, the theme remains the same. Write, enjoy what you write, write what you want to write, and defend your writing as stringently as you would defend an infant from a troll.

Is it hard? Yes, writing is often hard. It comes from who we are. But often the difficulties come from who we are as well. We let in the wrong advice; we don't remember that we're in charge of our own creativity; we let someone else's opinion matter more than our own.

If you take anything from this book, take these two things:

• You will have down times. Everyone does. You will take wrong paths. Everyone does. When you have a bad emotional reaction or a serious life crisis, then give yourself time to recover. When you get

knocked down, it's okay to lie on the floor for a while, as long as you get back up. You must always get back up.

• *Remember that your writing is* your *writing. You are responsible for your own career and your own creativity. That goes from setting habits to writing what* you *love.*

Good luck with your writing. Writing is, in my (clearly biased) opinion, the best job in the entire world.

Go forth, be creative—and most importantly, have fun.

ENDNOTES

Chapter One: Habits
1. Start with the post marked "Ghost Novel: Day 1," and read all of them. Here's the link for that post: http://www.deanwesleysmith. com/ghost-novel-day-1/

Chapter Two: The Importance of Routines
2. Click on any post marked "Writing in Public." http://www. deanwesleysmith.com/writing-in-public-year-2-month-9-day-10/

3. You can find *The Freelancer's Survival Guide* on my website for free, although it hasn't been updated or changed since I wrote those blogs. Here's the link to the free table of contents. I'd recommended the book, however, which is on its third edition. http://kriswrites. com/freelancers-survival-guide-table-of-contents/

Chapter Three: Churning It Out
4. This article, *A Billion-Dollar Affair,* appeared in *Entertainment Weekly* in the October 24, 2014, paper edition. Here's the link to the online version: http://www.ew.com/article/2014/10/17/ billion-dollar-affair

5. See my book *Discoverability* for more on these concepts, or find the relevant posts for free on my blog. http://kriswrites.com/ business-rusch-publishing-articles/discoverability-series/

6. For changes in traditional publishing at the end of 2014, including how the sales numbers for bestselling titles have declined, look here: http://kriswrites.com/2014/12/17/business-musings-what-traditional-publishing-learned-in-2014/

Chapter Four: Getting By
7. You can find all of our online workshops here: http://www.wmgpublishingworkshops.com

Chapter Six: Indispensable
8. I expanded on this post in the book, but here it is if you'd like to see the earlier draft. http://kriswrites.com/2014/01/29/the-business-rusch-marketing-and readers-discoverability-part-who-knows/

9. The post marked "Perfection" and the two business posts after it comprise most of the book *The Pursuit of Perfection*. http://kriswrites.com/2012/06/27/the-business-rusch-perfection/

Chapter Seven: Beginner's Luck
10. In the initial blog post, I named the contestant, who later left the show to go into rehab. He had other issues that had nothing to do with what I am dealing with in this chapter. Here's the information on him and his smart, healthy move: https://www.yahoo.com/music/anthony-riley-reveals-real-reason-for-leaving-the-114797006751.html

11. You can see the recap and video of that session here: http://ameristreamlive.com/ameristreamblog/2015/03/voice-battles-premiere-part-2/

12. You'll have to poke around Richie's website to find the video, since it comes and goes. (Or better yet, buy the CD.) Here's a link to the photo gallery, which does take you to the website: http://lionelrichie.com/galleries/tuskegee-3/

Chapter Eight: One Phone Call From Our Knees

13. You can still find the post on Dean's website if you follow this link: http://www.deanwesleysmith.com/personal-post-estate-done/

Chapter Nine: Controlling the Creatives

14. From *Rebus's Scotland: A Personal Journey* by Ian Rankin, Orion 2005.

Chapter Ten: Believe in Yourself

15. Here's the link to the NPR piece: http://www.npr.org/2011/11/10/141240217/my-accidental-masterpiece-the-phantom-tollbooth

16. I wrote the R*E*S*P*E*C*T after one of the worst experiences I'd ever had with an editor. Here's the link: http://kriswrites.com/2011/10/19/the-business-rusch-respect/. After that experience, I finished my project with that publishing house and asked to be released from the rest of my contract. Read the piece. What the editor put me through is horrible. What's worse is that she didn't get fired. In fact, as of this writing, she continues to treat authors like that each and every day.

Chapter Eleven: Out! All of You!

17. From *Lost Highway* by Peter Guralnick, Back Bay Books, 1999.

18. I can't locate what paper issue of *Vanity Fair* this quote is from, but you can find the entire nonfiction piece on Adam Levine at http://www.vanityfair.com/hollywood/2013/02/adam-levine-the-voice-character-damage

19. Sadly, the link no longer leads to the article on *RT*'s newly redesigned website. I'm afraid you'll have to look at back issues from around February 2013.

20. "Sally Field on the Journey from *Gidget* to *Lincoln*," *Nightline*, http://abcnews.go.com/Nightline/video/sally-field-journey-gidget-lincoln-18497175

21. "Bruce Willis' career is as indestructible as his 'Die-Hard' character," by Patrick Kevin Day, *Los Angeles Times*, February 19, 2013. http://articles.latimes.com/2013/feb/19/entertainment/la-et-mn-bruce-willis-20130219

22. "Ernest Tubb: The Texas Troubadour," Legacy.com. http://www.legacy.com/news/legends-and-legacies/ernest-tubb-the-texas-troubadour/232/

Chapter Twelve: The Writer You Want to Be
23. From Dean's blog series, *The New World of Publishing*: http://www.deanwesleysmith.com/the-new-world-of-publishing-what-should-indie-publishers-be-called/

24. "Editors & Publisher," by John McPhee, *The New Yorker*, July 2, 2012. http://www.newyorker.com/magazine/2012/07/02/editors-publisher

If you enjoyed *The Write Attitude*, you might also enjoy *The Pursuit of Perfection*, available now from your favorite bookseller.

Turn the page for a sample.

PERFECTION

At every craft workshop I teach, I make at least one writer cry. I wrote this chapter while teaching a short story workshop for professional writers. The writers who attend are workshop-hardened folk, people who have been eviscerated by the best of them, people who come to my workshops having heard that I make writers cry, expecting me to be the most vicious critiquer of all.

How do I bring writers to tears? Usually by saying this:

I loved this story. It's wonderful. Mail it.

That's my entire critique.

Is the story perfect? Of course not. No story is. Not a one. No matter how many times it's "polished" and "fixed" and "improved." No one can write a perfect story.

If such a thing existed, then we would all read the same books and enjoy them equally. We would watch the same movies and need reviewers to tell us only which movie is perfect and which one isn't. We would buy the same comics, again, going only for the comic that is perfect, and ignoring all the others.

Am I telling people to write crap? No. Because the choice isn't between crap and perfection. Those are false choices.

I learned this lesson long ago. Dean Wesley Smith and I were visitors at a writing workshop taught by science fiction writer and editor Algis Budrys. One of the early volumes of *Writers of the Future*, which he had edited, had just appeared, and he asked the students to read one of the stories in the volume.

Then, without telling Dean and me what he was doing, he asked us to comment on the story.

Here's what I remember of the piece: It was 2,000 words long. I think we spoke more than 2,000 words in our elegant, impressive critiques.

Algis looked at both of us sadly. Then he said, "Ignore them. The story is wonderful—or at least it is to this editor."

He had expected us to praise the story, thinking we all had the same taste. Instead, Dean and I both had gone after the story in critique mode. When a reader critiques something, he goes after it by searching for what is wrong.

And he will find something. Something is always wrong. From an infelicitous turn of phrase to a plot point that could have been stronger, something about the story does not work.

As I'm teaching this concept to my workshop-experienced students, I always begin by asking them this, "What's wrong with Shakespeare's *A Midsummer Night's Dream*?"

Well, we're all raised to believe that Shakespeare is a god who never could do *anything* wrong. Had he done anything wrong, had his stories been less-than-perfect, we wouldn't be reading them? Right?

Wrong.

If William Shakespeare—professional writer—had turned *A Midsummer Night's Dream* in at a workshop I taught, I would have told him this:

"Bill, lose at least two of your endings. The main story of the play ends in Act IV, Scene 2—and then you go on for two more scenes. All of these endings would work. Pick one."

Bill Shakespeare, dutiful workshopper that he is, would nod sadly, go back to his room, and delete one of the most favorite and quoted scenes in all of English literature. Puck turns to the audience and says,

If we shadows have offended,
Think but this, and all is mended,
That you have but slumber'd here
While these visions did appear.

I would have said to Bill, "Lovely. Thematically significant. Beautifully written. Lose it. You can do the same thing elsewhere."

Yeah, right. My harsh words, spoken with authority, and Workshopper Bill's insecurity would have stolen 400 years of enjoyment from audiences all over the world.

Anything can be critiqued. Criticizing something is *easy*. It makes the critiquer feel smart, and just a little bit superior to the writer.

But that kind of critique serves no real purpose, because that kind of critique is wrong from the moment the critiquer picks up the story or the manuscript or the 400-year-old play.

Readers read for enjoyment. They vote for what they like with their cold hard cash. Traditional publishers who recently ventured into the world of free online e-book promotions were stunned to realize that people who receive a book for free are more apt to write a vicious, nasty review of that book than people who paid money for the same book.

There are a few reasons for that. One is that people see no value in something they get for free.

But the one reason that's relevant to this essay is this: If people have paid a little for a book, they have a vested interest in it. They take a small bit of the blame if the reading experience didn't turn out exactly like they hoped. They should have looked at the cover more closely, perhaps, or read a snippet of the opening. But they didn't. So they got a book they didn't like. It was an accident. They'll do better next time.

Readers are more realistic than writers. Readers understand that many books out there in the universe won't be to their taste. All sorts of marketing tools have sprung up over the centuries to help readers find works that will be to their taste. From cover art to genre categories to back cover blurbs, all these things exist to help a reader choose the right book for them—a book they won't regret purchasing. A book they will *enjoy*.

When a reader samples an e-book, she gets a small portion of the novel. If it's to her taste, she will then decide whether or not to purchase. But if the book is really, really good, the reader will punch that "buy" button just to see what happens next regardless of price. (That's how a lot of e-books priced over $10 sell to people who swear they'll never pay more than $9.99 for an e-book. The reader samples, gets hooked, and buys, without checking price at all.)

What does that have to do with critique? Simple. Critiquers get the manuscript for free *and they're asked to criticize it*. Of course, they will find something wrong with it. In that circumstance, we all will.

So I change my students' mindset to a reader/editor mindset. How do I do it? By giving them only three valid responses to something they've read:

1. I liked what I read.
2. I quit on page [insert number here].
3. I liked what I read and I would have bought this.

Book and magazine editors don't have time to read every manuscript that crosses their desks, and certainly don't have time to critique them. Editors want to find something the readers will enjoy. Better yet, the editors want those people to return for a second bite from the apple. So they want the readers to enjoy the first book, and come back for the second by the same author. In fact, the editors want readers to return to the publishing house again and again, which is why imprints exist. (If you liked this book by Suzy Q. Writer, then try this book by Jane X. Author, published under the same imprint.)

In other words, editors also read for enjoyment. And if they're not enjoying a book on page 2, they'll jettison that book. The only time they use their editing superpowers on that book is if they bought it sight unseen from a professional writer and can't reject it for cause. Then they try to help the writer "improve" that book, when really, if the editor were an average reader, he would have simply tossed the book aside and asked for another book (maybe even by somebody else).

Harsh? Not really. Not compared to a thirty-minute critique of a romance novel by a hard-science fiction writer forced to read said romance novel as part of a workshop. You ain't heard harsh until then.

But I'm sure all you writers out there have heard just such a critique. And many of you have taken it to heart. I know dozens of writers who quit writing because they couldn't stand the pain they received from their peer-level writing workshop. That's a tragedy. How many stories have we lost? How many Bill Shakespeares have dumped the "unnecessary" second and third endings from their immensely enjoyable stories because some idiot told them to?

I don't let students drone on and on about a story, *especially* if they don't like it. I will occasionally give the student something to improve the story, but before I do, I remind the student that 1) My word has equal weight to every other reader's word in the room; 2) I can be wrong; and 3) ignore everything I say if you disagree with me.

I go last, after I've heard the rest of the workshop. If anyone "buys" the manuscript at all and I didn't like the manuscript or had found "flaws," I remind the writer that someone already loved it and was willing to spend cold, hard cash on it.

Often, I tell writers this: *Do not touch this story. Mail it. Everyone in the room liked it but me. Therefore what I have to say is irrelevant.*

In other words, I never tell a student to make a story perfect. I often tell a student that the story is really good and needs to get out into the world where readers can find it.

I also teach writers bits and pieces of craft, things they might not be aware of. I don't want them to create *my* perfect story. I want them to write stories that only they can tell.

So many writers table perfectly good stories because someone—often someone with power (an editor, a writer with a few novels under her belt, a well-published nonfiction writer)—will nitpick the story to death. Or suggest revisions that will alter the story dramatically. If the story already works, who cares if it has three endings? Those of us who don't like the story don't know if the people who loved the story loved it *because* of those three endings, not in spite of them.

When I became an editor, I learned just how important taste is. The difference between the short stories in *Analog* and *Asimov's*, two of the science fiction digest magazines (that now have e-book editions each month if you haven't seen them before), isn't that there is such thing as an *Analog* story or an *Asimov's* story that I as a long-time reader can tell you about. The difference is in the taste of their editors. Trevor Quachri of *Analog* likes different kinds of stories than Sheila Williams of *Asimov's* does. Occasionally their tastes overlap. Most often, they do not.

If there were such a thing as a perfect sf story, then both editors would always buy the same stories, and you couldn't tell the magazines apart.

As readers, you all know this. As writers, you forget it.

And when you forget it, you make the weirdest decisions.

You give control of your product to the wrong people. You submit romance novels to science fiction markets (and wonder why the editor didn't read your manuscript—was it the passive sentence on page 32?). You try to revise to please everyone in your peer-level writing group.

You self-publish your novel, make sure it's edited and copy-edited, add a fantastic cover, and *then revise to address concerns posted by reviewers who gave your book one star.* That's complete and utter idiocy. Seriously.

Some nutty brand new writer with one or two novels to her name posted a blog on Digital Book World espousing just that. She says writers should always address their critics' concerns.

I read that and nearly snorted my tea all over my iPad. If I even tried to address all the nasty reviews I've gotten over the years, I'd never write anything new. If I tried to address all the somewhat valid criticisms I've gotten on my books, I'd still spend forever revising.

Only a writer with one or two publications to her credit would have time to even think such a thing is viable.

Her blog post has gone viral, and I've seen new writers everywhere wring their hands over the fact that they now have to pay attention to their one-star reviews and constantly revise.

I'm here to tell you this: If you want a career as a writer, ignore your critics.

When the book is finished, when the book is *published* for heaven's sake, then it's done. Irrevocably done. Mistakes and all.

And there will be mistakes. Lots of them.

One of my copy editors has been comparing my final manuscripts to the previously published editions of my novels as a final prep for the books' reissues. She's done that for two years now, and she's found many things that copy editors missed. (Failing to capitalize Diet Coke in a novel published by Dell, for instance.) We're fixing those tiny copyediting things because WMG Publishing is reissuing the books. Reissues always need proofs as they go into a new format because the format itself can introduce errors.

But she's been having fits over one of the latest two Grayson novels, which will be reissued this summer. She complained in person to me about it. I frowned and said that I seemed to recall a bad copyedit on one of the Grayson books.

She wrote an e-mail to me later saying, "You really did have a horrible [copy] editor on this one. S/he/it (and yes, that really does say a lot about it) faithfully reproduced nearly every misspelled word, and introduced some errors...in the ms. Yeesh!"

In other words, the entire book was riddled with typos—and yes, we're fixing them. But am I taking the opportunity to revise the book? No, I'm not. The book stands as it did when I originally wrote it. Readers loved those books. I'm not going to try to invalidate their reading experience by "improving" on it. I might take out the thing that they love.

A writer whose work I adore has revised my favorite novel of hers twice, publishing each revision as a new edition, *neither of which I will buy*. I loved that first edition of that book. I don't care how much better she's gotten as a craftsperson. That book didn't need a word changed, in my opinion.

At the workshop, one of the students pre-critiqued his own manuscript right after I called his name. We were well into the workshop by then; the writers knew the drill. We'd talk about the manuscript and then the author could speak. But he picked up the manuscript and volunteered to throw it away before we could comment on it.

Another student turned on him and growled, "I *loved* this story." Then everyone else piled on. Yep, most of us had loved that story and all of us who had loved it were deeply offended that he thought it flawed.

When you learn a new bit of craft, when your skills have improved, when a reader points out a valid storytelling mistake in your published book that would take a complete revision of that book, what should you do?

Leave the book alone.

Incorporate what you've learned into the next book. You'll learn something new on that book that you can then incorporate into the *next* book. Keep writing, keep learning, keep improving. But for God's sake, don't look backwards. Those books are done.

How do you know when a manuscript is done? That's trickier. I think you should trust the process, fix the nits, and move to the next book. Writing is a subconscious art, not a conscious one. You heard your first story before you could speak, so your subconscious knows a lot more about writing than your conscious brain ever will.

Trust that.

Many writers don't believe what I just wrote, and that's fine. You need to define it for yourself. Set a limit on revisions, set a limit on drafts, set a time limit. (My book must be done in August, no matter what.) Then release your book on the unsuspecting public.

The book will never be perfect. Take the advice that those of us who've worked in broadcasting learned long ago. I think it was best expressed by Tina Fey in *Bossy Pants:* The show doesn't go on when it's finished; it goes on because it's 11:30.

Exactly. At some point, you must simply let go of that book or story or play and move to the next.

If our workshopping friend Bill Shakespeare strove for perfection, we would never have heard of him. We wouldn't have gotten all of that marvelous writing, all of those wonderful—flawed—

plays. (You don't think *A Midsummer Night's Dream* is the only one riddled with possible workshop-identifiable errors, do you? Think of *Romeo and Juliet*. Why didn't those crazy lovesick kids just move to another town????)

With so many publishing options, it's harder now for a writer to believe in her work. Does she go to traditional publishing and ask them to validate her book? Does she self-publish and hope for the best?

I understand that. I also think that writers need to understand that they're not writing for one editor or agent or for a small subset of people like a critique group. Writers write for *readers*.

And it's up to the writer as to how to find those readers. As Sarah A. Hoyt said in last week's comments, ask yourself, "How will this book best reach its audience?" The key words here are "book," "reach," and "audience."

Not "How do I impress Editor A?" or "How do I get an agent?" But how does *this book* best reach *its* audience? Sometimes that answer is through traditional publishing. Sometimes that answer is to become an indie writer.

The question should never ever be, "How do I write the perfect novel?" because the perfect novel or short story or play or article or essay *does not exist*.

A better question is, "How do I make the book the best it can be?" That you have to answer for yourself. Me, I make sure I have outside help—a dedicated first reader or two or three *before* my book goes to my editor in traditional publishing or to the people I hire when I self-publish. A copy editor in both cases to make sure that my dyslexia doesn't make my books impossible to read. A "stet" stamp so that I can disagree with said copy editor when I wanted a particular misspelling or poorly constructed sentence to stand *for story reasons*. The best possible cover. The best possible interior design.

Sometimes I get a say in those last two things. Sometimes I don't.

I also don't always get a say in how the books get distributed either. Remember, my goal is to find my audience, and when my traditional publishers choose not to pursue every distribution option open to them (because it's too much work or there's "too little return"), I get angry.

My readership varies from book to book, series to series, genre to genre. I never know who will like something I wrote. I just have to give that person the opportunity to find what I did.

Sometimes readers like my work. Sometimes they don't. Once the book is released into the wilds of publishing, however, it's done. Finished. I will not revise a published book.

Is my craft better than it was twenty years ago when I published my first novel? Oh, hell, yes. But my craft is so much better that I could never have written that novel now. Because there's something in the middle of it that no established writer, steeped in craft, would ever attempt. At the time I wrote the book, I didn't know you couldn't do that thing, so I did it.

Had I workshopped that novel, more experienced writers would have told me to remove that thing. Yet that thing is what readers remark on the most about that novel.

When you strive for perfection in your writing, you're dooming yourself to perpetual failure. When you strive to be the best you can be, you will have a fulfilling life.

Writers who are always improving, always learning, move forward. They are secure in the knowledge that the book they wrote ten years ago is the best book it could have been given their level of craft and their understanding of the art of writing *at the time they finished the book*. They're better now, so they write new things, explore new pathways.

They grow.

They also realize that they have a *career*, not a novel. The people who tell you to endlessly revise, the people who tell you not to try something new until you've mastered the old, the people who believe that you should make every word perfect before you move onto a new project, those people don't have writing careers. They might have things that *seem* like writing careers, like a few published stories, one or two novels.

But they don't make their living from their craft (in other words, publishing their writing). They also approach storytelling from the point of view of *perfection*, not the point of view of *enjoyment*.

If a flawed novel entertains, it has done its job.

How do you know if a novel entertains? Talk to its fans. Look at its sales figures. See how many people recommend it to their friends.

How do you learn to be the best writer you can be? Step one: Read other people's work *for enjoyment*. Stop critiquing manuscripts. Stop thinking everything can be perfect.

Then write a lot. Practice, practice, practice. Find your audience—and *respect them*.

After all, they're forking out their hard-earned cash to pay for one of your stories. If they buy more of your work, then you're doing something right.

Perfection in publishing—like perfection in life—does not exist.

So why do people cry in my craft workshops? Essentially because I tell them they don't have to be perfect. They just need to have fun. They need to share that fun with their readers. Writers understand that. We all do. We like to share our work—the best work we can do—with other people. Not perfect work. The best. Even if it has two additional unnecessary endings.

Like this.

To read more, pick up a copy of *The Pursuit of Perfection* from your favorite retailer.

ABOUT THE AUTHOR

International bestselling writer Kristine Kathryn Rusch has won or been nominated for every major award in the science fiction field. She has won Hugos for editing *The Magazine of Fantasy & Science Fiction* and for her short fiction. She has also won the *Asimov's Science Fiction Magazine* Readers Choice Award six times, as well as the Anlab Award from *Analog Magazine*, *Science Fiction Age* Readers Choice Award, the Locus Award, and the John W. Campbell Award. Her standalone sf novel, *Alien Influences*, was a finalist for the prestigious Arthur C. Clarke Award. *Io9* said her Retrieval Artist series featured one of the top ten science fiction detectives ever written. She writes a second sf series, the Diving Universe series, as well as a fantasy series called The Fey. She also writes mystery, romance and fantasy novels, occasionally using the pen names Kris DeLake, Kristine Grayson and Kris Nelscott. For more information about her work, or to sign up for her newsletter, go to kristinekathrynrusch.com.

Printed in Great Britain
by Amazon.co.uk, Ltd.,
Marston Gate.